The Road
of
Blessing

FINDING GOD'S DIRECTION
FOR YOUR LIFE

Penelope Wilcock

MONARCH
BOOKS

Oxford, UK & Grand Rapids, Michigan, USA

First published in the UK in 2011 by Monarch Books
(a publishing imprint of Lion Hudson plc)
Wilkinson House, Jordan Hill Road, Oxford OX2 8DR, England
Tel: +44 (0)1865 302750 Fax: +44 (0)1865 302757
Email: monarch@lionhudson.com www.lionhudson.com

ISBN 978 1 85424 965 4

Distributed by:
UK: Marston Book Services, PO Box 269, Abingdon, Oxon, OX14 4YN
USA: Kregel Publications, PO Box 2607, Grand Rapids, Michigan 49501

British Library Cataloguing Data
A catalogue record for this book is available from the British Library.

Printed and bound in the UK by CPI Cox & Wyman, Reading.

For my friend Joan Leyland ('Emle'), who blesses

us all just by being here.

Never was there a gentler or kinder soul.

Contents

Foreword   7

Acknowledgments   11

Chapter One:
What Does it Mean to Follow the Road of Blessing?   13

Chapter Two:
How Do We Recognize the Road of Blessing?   27

Chapter Three:
Understanding the Power of Blessing   63

Chapter Four:
Stepping Stones on the Road of Blessing   111

Questions and Answers   170

Foreword

Okay. When you write a book, whether someone came looking for you to write it, or you proposed it through an agent, or you are famous enough to turn up out of the blue with a manuscript, slap it down on a desk in an office somewhere and say: 'Interested?' – there is still a process to go through.

Even if your agent is nodding sagely and tapping his nose with his finger saying, 'I'm sure we can place this one'; even if a little flame is kindling in the commissioning editor's eyes ('I think maybe we've got something here…'), so that you feel certain 'Yes! yes! yes!' is surely forthcoming; there are hurdles. There are still hurdles. There are editorial committees and marketing men, there are meetings behind closed doors when decisions are made by men far too cool to wear suits and women with calm appraising eyes and a no-nonsense manner. 'No! no! no!' may still be forthcoming.

Like you, I dream the world. I turn things over in my head, and I mosey along wondering why I'm alive and looking into the Gospel like someone gazing into a clear lake, looking past what is only my own reflection and the clouds behind me to see the life and beauty hidden in its depths. Every now and then, I see something move, and I feel the reality of it, and I start to live it in the everyday; touch the live pulse of something that is more than a theory or a doctrine. A defining truth that gives structure and meaning to the relative chaos of my life.

Then, when I've been on that trail for a while, and I know it works; know the truth of it down to the soles of my feet, know I can trust it – I want to share it. I don't mean just a bright idea: I mean the sort of truth you can trust so completely that you can rely on it for your income; the sort of truth you can trust your children to; truth that you can lean on when you have to decide who to marry and how to live.

I don't always notice the principle forming at first. I get on the scent of it, follow it along, dream it and ponder it, turn it over and over, live into it and get familiar with it – and only then do I notice: 'Hey! Wait a minute! This is something you may like to know about too!'

That's how *The Road of Blessing* came to be written.

It all started when I was chatting to my trusty editor about the business plans of a mutual friend. I said I was worried about her taking out a loan. I thought she needed to play things safe, as it could all very well go pear-shaped because she wasn't following the road of blessing. And he looked at me blankly and said those magical words: 'What do you mean?'

Then, when I went to open a new bank account so that someone who had gulled me for rather a large sum of money could pay it back, I got chatting to the bank lady, who asked me what I do for a living. When I said, 'I'm a writer,' she wanted to know all about the book I'd most recently written (so I told her), then all about the book I would be writing next.

Never, never tell people about the book you will be writing next. Never. Once you've told someone what's going to be in that book, you won't need to write it, and the flame in you will just die down to ashes. So I didn't tell her what would be in it. I only said, 'Well, it's a book that explains how to live your life successfully, so that things go well instead of messing up all the time. It explains the principles that govern what makes things go well, and where you can find them in the Bible.'

She sat up very straight, looked at me with shining eyes, and said: 'I need that book!'

Meanwhile, behind closed doors in that office somewhere, the men who are too cool to wear suits and the no-nonsense women with the calm appraising eyes, were mulling over my proposal.

They saw the word 'blessing', and they saw that my trusty editor had explained: 'This is not the same as "Prosperity Gospel" teaching', but it set all their alarm bells clanging.

'We do not – *not* –' (they came back to us) 'want to publish a Prosperity Gospel book. You'll have to send in two sample chapters.'

Well, that was okay, because I knew that this book had to be written. When the still small voice of the Spirit is whispering, when you want to teach other people about the way of the Gospel, when you are touching upon the truth that sets you free – I mean, there isn't going to be a problem over a publisher, is there? It will find its own way up into the light. I know that, like the bank lady, you will need this book.

You will have seen – go on, I'm *sure* you have – one of those dusty places by the roadside where they laid a heavy, tarry, pitch-black layer of tarmac. If you tried to dig it up with a garden fork, you'd only bend the tines. If you tried to scratch it up with your bare hands, you'd only hurt yourself. But there is something pushing the surface up into a little hump, cracking it open, splitting it right apart: a tiny, tender, soft, green, little plant, that you could bruise and crush and kill between two fingers. What is that power but the power of the Holy Spirit in a living thing: actually unstoppable.

So I hadn't too many worries about what I have to say here finding its way to the light: it will do, by one means or another. It's my privilege if it happens to be through me.

And, no – this is *not* a Prosperity Gospel book.

This is a book for people who are willing to understand how to be happy in the lowest place, for people who are content to walk the badger tracks and find their peace in simplicity. This arises from the wisdom of Jesus Christ, who went the dusty way, the quiet way, the mountain way, in his sandals and his homespun robe.

We are talking about following the way of blessing.

My prayer for you is that its freedom and peace will refresh the roots of your soul. May the Spirit within you well up to a fountain of living water; may the Way open to you, and may you learn to trust it. It will never fail you.

Acknowledgments

I am indebted to the Reverend Canon Martin Baddeley, who was Principal of the Southwark Ordination Course when I trained to be a minister of religion, for three things especially.

The first is that he is the person who taught me always to approach the scriptures holding in mind the question: 'What kind of God?' This question is vital in establishing scriptural *principle* and avoiding sterile legalism.

The second is that, though identifying 'sandwiches' as a Markan technique of presenting a story is commonplace, it was Martin Baddeley whose teaching opened my eyes to the 'sandwich' *structure* of Mark's gospel, and showed me that the entire literary composition of that gospel is pressed into the service of communicating its essential message. I have added thoughts of my own, and developed the idea to the form in which it is presented here, but the germ of it came from Martin.

The third is that during the course of my years on the Southwark Ordination Course, unusual circumstances created a situation of transition requiring administrative changes that generated a strong swell of internal politics. I was privileged to be there to see Martin handle with such extraordinary grace and humility a cast of attitude and a series of events that should never have have happened. His gentleness and willingness to take the lowest place and work unswervingly for his students and his Master won my respect, my esteem. He already had my love, because of his kindness and the prayer in which his life was steeped.

I should also here acknowledge that I first learned that we have the power to effect blessing in our lives and the lives of others by our words and actions from Timothy Pain, in the context of the Ashburnham Stable family, in his Signs and Wonders teaching courses during the 1980s. It was there that I realized for the first time that our words have actual power – not the ordinary psychological or emotional power we all know about, but *spiritual* power: the power of the Making. I also learned from Tim the principle that a curse needs a foothold in a person's life; that evil could never ultimately overcome Jesus because it had no foothold in him (Ephesians 4:27; John 14:30; Acts 2:24; 1 Thessalonians 5:21). I learned that this is the value of a blameless and holy life; it offers the individual protection in their circumstances, however grim those may be. For this reason, our integrity is a priceless possession; as soon as we lose it, we become dreadfully vulnerable – and this is why we stand in desperate need of the protective clothing of God's forgiveness in Christ.

My grateful thanks are also due to those kind friends who read through the manuscript for me and furnished me with the questions for the last section of the book: John and Rosanna Walton, Alice and Hebe Wilcock, Gail Trussler and Julie Balmer. You did a grand job and I am immensely grateful. Thank you so much.

Chapter One

What Does it Mean to Follow the Road of Blessing?

First of all; it doesn't seem to matter at what point you join the road. If there are aspects of this Way that you struggle with – forgiveness, maybe; or trust, or letting go – there is no need to agonize over it. In time, it will come to you; the way will open.

If you read through chapters 9–11 of Luke's gospel, an amazing adventure of Spirit-filled ministry unfolds before you.

The Twelve are given authority by Jesus to heal the sick and cast out demons, to live by faith and preach the Kingdom. Wherever they go, people are healed – word even reaches Herod, people think maybe John the Baptist has been raised from the dead! Then comes the feeding of the five thousand (a disciples' miracle – Jesus blessed and broke the bread, but the disciples fed the people) and then the transfiguration (when the glory that was in Jesus blazed out visibly, and his disciples caught a glimpse of his wondrous light and power). After that, come arguments and failure and lots of teaching taken on board. They experience rejection and volunteer to call down fire from heaven in retribution, but Jesus says, 'Er – no!'

Their ranks are swelled and seventy-two go out on the next signs-and-wonders tour. They return with joy, reporting that even demons submit to them. Jesus rejoices at the power of the Spirit filling them: 'I have given you authority to...

overcome all the power of the enemy; nothing will harm you' (Luke 10:19). That's *amazing*!

They travel on, the crowd swells, Jesus teaches and tells stories.

And then – only *then* – one of his disciples turns to him and says, 'Lord – teach us to pray.'

What happened to the golden rule every church leader knows, that without prayer you can't even open the church council or eat your tea, never mind cast out a demon or heal an incurable disease?

This demonstrates that there is no right order to do things in. The road of blessing is holistic. You don't have to work your way up through the ranks. God meets you where you are and puts into your hands whatever you are ready for – generously, unstintingly, joyously.

A friend of mine graduated from university knowing he wanted to teach, but feeling ready for, and drawn to, teaching only older students: 16-to-18-year-olds. When he applied for teaching jobs, they laughed at him. 'Oh, sure! We all want to teach the older students, it's more rewarding. But *we* had to work our way up, and start at the bottom with the little kids, and so will *you*!' Tough on my friend, tougher still on the little kids, and badly irrational. But God is not the County Council Education Department Board. He has no pecking orders; you start with what you are ready for, you begin where you are. Wherever and whoever you are, however much or little faith you have, you can start right in.

But though it doesn't matter where you join the road or how you make a start, it matters very much that you do actually begin. These are the strongest things in life:

- The Name of Jesus.
- The energy of the Holy Spirit.
- Truth spoken in the innocence of a child.
- Habit.

As following the road of blessing becomes a habit in your life, though it continues to be costly it begins to sit easy on you: 'For my yoke is easy, and my burden is light' (Matthew 11:30).

There is a sense in which force of habit carried Jesus through Gethsemane, his trial and the cross: by the time he had got that far, he would not have known how else to be but the way he was, what else to say but the truth, how else to respond but with faithfulness, authority and love. Jesus always walked in the will of God; his feet knew no other way to go.

When we begin following in the road of blessing, there are old habits and patterns of thought and speech to be broken; and new habits to form. They have to be laid down layer by layer, patiently; becoming second nature and then, over time, our actual nature – the people we have become. The way to form a habit is to begin.

So, on the understanding that we can join the road of blessing at whatever point we find ourselves, and that the important thing is to make a beginning, let's look now at the concepts and principles involved.

The first principle is that there is a pattern to life: it is orderly, not random. 'Chance', 'luck', 'happenstance', 'mere coincidence' are interpretations put upon events by people with an incomplete grasp of what is happening to them, and an unwillingness or inability to create a habit of seeing what we believe instead of believing what we see. Life is intentional, meaningful. The universe is flowing in a particular direction

– the direction of God's will. 'We know that all things work together for good for those who love God and are called according to his purpose' (Romans 8:28, my paraphrase).

The letter to the Colossians speaks of the essential unity, or integrity, of all created things:

> [Christ] is before all things, and in him all things hold together. And he is the head of the body, the church; he is the beginning and the firstborn from among the dead, so that in everything he might have the supremacy. For God was pleased to have all his fulness dwell in him, and through him to reconcile to himself all things, whether things on earth or things in heaven, by making peace through his blood, shed on the cross.
>
> *Colossians 1:17–20*

This means that everything that is co-exists in a single organic unity orchestrated and nourished by Christ. His atoning death on the cross has resulted in absolutely everything now being at one (that's what atonement – at-one-ment – is). The cross of Christ is at the heart of creation, holding all things together: and the spiritual victory of his sacrifice has brought about an imperishable and eternal healing, not to humankind only but to the whole of creation – to the entirety of the way things are.

The road of blessing is created by this underlying framework of reality. It is there because God the creator is there. Like a spider spinning her web from the substance of her own body, God spins or breathes or sings out of his own *ruach* every created thing.

Ruach is a Hebrew word that crops up in the Old Testament. It can mean 'wind' or 'spirit' or 'breath'. This multi-meaning allows us to access an understanding that the spiritual and physical are not really separate. They are at the same time one and not-one. So of course we see quickly that a soul is not the same as a body – and yet separating the two means death.

I am using this rather clumsy term 'not-one', instead of saying 'two', because 'two' implies the possibility of duality, of separating right out. We are never separated completely from God or each other. We are never 'two':

> For I am convinced that neither death nor life, neither
> angels nor demons, neither the present nor the future, nor
> any powers, neither height nor depth, nor anything else
> in all creation, will be able to separate us from the love of
> God that is in Christ Jesus our Lord.
>
> *Romans 8:38–39*

Duality does not apply. Even so, it is possible to see that there are times when we are in disharmony with ourselves, each other and God; there are times when we are attempting to travel against the flow of God's blessing; there are times when we feel far away from God; and we do each have our own unique and individual being. So we are one, yet not-one.

The word *ruach* comes right at the beginning of the Bible:

> Now the earth was formless [*tohu*, confused] and empty
> [*bohu*, desolate, waste], darkness was over the surface of
> the deep, and the Spirit [*ruach*] of God [*Elohim*, a plural
> form that takes a singular verb – the first implication, for
> Christians, of the Trinity] was hovering over the waters.
>
> *Genesis 1:2*

However, when God creates Adam, the story (Genesis 2:7) says: 'the Lord God formed the man from the dust of the ground and breathed into his nostrils the breath of life, and the man became a living being', and the Hebrew word used here for God breathing into Adam is not *ruach*.

This verse, so rich in understanding, says that God breathed (*napach*: a puff of breath, like the kiss of life) into Adam the breath (*nÿshamah*: a big word implying what is necessary for survival, and meaning the breath of God, humanity and every living thing) of life (*chay*: another huge word, incorporating the coming of life again in the springtime; community; the freshness of life in green and growing things and flowing water; family, liveliness; sustenance and maintenance).

The name 'Adam' is a play on the Hebrew word *adamah*, meaning 'earthy'. So the name is like 'Earthling'. Adam is made from the dust of the ground – *aphar* – debris, rubbish, dust; but when God breathes into him, he becomes a *nephesh* – a soul, a person, with desires and emotions and passions.

We don't get to know Eve's name until chapter 4, but her name means 'life'. Earthy and Life – what an amazing marriage!

So the understanding is that us being alive at all, everything about us that is anything more than the rubble and dust of the contents of a cremation urn, is because of the breath of God in us. We are all the sons and daughters of Earthy and Life, and we are animated (another interesting word, from the Latin *anima*, meaning 'soul') and sustained by the breath of God.

Then as we move through the Old Testament, we keep coming across the word *ruach*, which fills out for us our understanding of what the breath of God might be.

I think it's important to realize that there is more here than just metaphor. 'Metaphor' implies that something is like something else, as when the Psalmist says, 'O Lord my rock'. He doesn't mean God is a pebble; he means the qualities of strength, dependability and endurance that he experiences in God are reminiscent of rock. But when we talk about the breath of God in us giving us life, this is first cause, not secondary resemblance.

God is spirit, and breath is physical, so this could be puzzling for us. It helps to think of how light works: white light contains all the colours in itself, and it is when light is split through a prism that the colours become visible. So the white light, in which all colours are implicit but not manifest, is like spirit, in which all the physical forms and energies of creation are implicit but not manifest. We can think of God in terms of radiance, pouring forth light ('In him was life, and that life was the light of men... the true light that gives light to every man was coming into the world', John 1:4, 9), and that the light becomes visible as it takes physical form in all its multiplicity.

For the sake of accuracy, we should pause to note that we cannot reduce the being of God simply to 'light', but light is a very primal manifestation of God: 'God is light; in him there is no darkness at all' (1 John 1:5); 'He wraps himself in light as with a garment' (Psalm 104:2); 'And God said, "Let there be light," and there was light' (Genesis 1:3; this is God's primary word).

The word *ruach* is used in Ezekiel's story of the Valley of the Dry Bones (Ezekiel 37). God shows Ezekiel the scattered bones of the dead in a dry valley, and calls him to prophesy to the bones, asking him, 'Can these bones live?' Ezekiel does as he has been told, and the bones eerily reassemble into corpses. Then God says:

> 'Prophesy to the breath [*ruach*]; prophesy, son of man, and say to it, "This is what the Sovereign Lord says: Come from the four winds [*ruach*], O breath [*ruach*], and breathe [*napach* – like God breathing into Adam] into these slain, that they may live."' So I prophesied as he commanded me, and breath [*ruach*] entered them; they came to life and stood up on their feet – a vast army.
>
> *Ezekiel 37:9–10*

We come across the *ruach* in Psalm 104, a wonderful song of amazing breadth and vision, that expounds and rejoices in the involvement of God in creation. The psalmist vividly describes the teeming world of living things in all its richness and variety – everything from mountain goats to whales to wind and fire. Then he says:

> These all look to you to give them their food at the proper time… When you hide your face, they are terrified; when you take away their breath [*ruach*], they die and return to the dust. When you send your Spirit [*ruach*], they are created, and you renew the face of the earth.
>
> *Psalm 104:27, 29–30*

This gives us an image of the living and dying of all creatures, the ebbing and flowing of all life, as being like God breathing in and out.

It accords well with what Isaiah says about the changing fortunes of our lives: 'I form the light and create darkness, I bring prosperity and create disaster; I, the Lord, do all these

20

things' (Isaiah 45:7). Once we understand this, we see that death as much as life, disaster as much as prosperity, are part of the road of blessing, because they come from God and are consistent with his presence and the flow of his desire, his will.

Isaiah goes on to say, in the next chapter: 'Even to your old age and grey hairs I am he, I am he who will sustain you. I have made you and I will carry you; I will sustain you and I will rescue you' (Isaiah 46:4).

So the first principle implicit in the concept of the road of blessing is that there is a God, who created all things, and whose Spirit or breath holds all things in being. The created things are not God, yet are not separate from God – God and they are one but not-one – because without the breath or Spirit of God in them, they would be no more than dust.

This means that we can be confident that our lives are governed by loving intelligence, that they hold together with all created things, that they are in origin and nature spiritual; and that because of the *ruach* of God, and the cross of Christ at the heart of creation, though everything has its own separate form and being, they are all connected with each other and with God – not-one but one. So we do not worship Nature, but all of creation is holy.

This connection means that anything can be a doorway into God for us, a stepping stone onto the road of blessing: 'For since the creation of the world God's invisible qualities – his eternal power and divine nature – have been clearly seen, being understood from what has been made' (Romans 1:20). The stepping stone is not the whole journey: if we content ourselves with nature-worship or hedonism or politics or personal religion, even though we touch God in that aspect of his radiance, that colour in the spectrum of his greater light, we are limiting both our experience and our contribution – both what God has in store for us and what we are here to do. But any aspect of life can be our starting point, because God's *ruach* breathes in all of life, and his love is at work in all our circumstances.

Creation is alive, not fixed: it is dynamic, not static. It is not neutral, it is God-breathed and God-orientated (see Psalms 19:1–4; 104; 148 etc.). It is flowing, directional – there is a current to it. This is the heart of the road of blessing – realizing that there is a definite direction to move in, which makes a difference to our quality of life, because it is the flow of the Spirit.

Because we are made in the image of God, it is in our nature to return to God, to go God's way. This is what Jesus meant when he said: "'Shew me a penny. Whose image and superscription hath it?" They answered and said, "Caesar's". And he said unto them, "Render therefore unto Caesar the things which be Caesar's, and unto God the things which be God's'" (Luke 20:24–25 KJV). What is made in God's image (*we* are) should always be returned again to him.

The *ruach* of God is what makes each of us a *nephesh*, a living being, not just a lump of matter: it is impossible for us to get away from God, because our very nature comes from God – and not only our nature, but *all* nature. For this reason, though it is sometimes costly and demanding to follow in the road of blessing, not to do so is to act against our own nature and all the rest of nature. When we do not travel in the road of blessing, it's like rubbing our fur the wrong way.

Just as 'all things work together for good for those who love God' (Romans 8:28, my paraphrase), so correspondingly all things continually act to trip you up and frustrate you when you travel outside the will of God. This is still true even if you are rich and successful: peace and contentment belong to the road of blessing.

This does not mean that peace and contentment are experienced only by religious people, or that all Christian people inevitably experience peace and contentment: it depends on following the road of blessing. Remember that you can join the road at any point. You might acquiesce to Christian creeds and doctrines, but if you are not following in the Way, you will not experience peace and contentment. Jesus put it like this:

> Thus, by their fruit you will recognise them. Not everyone
> who says to me, 'Lord, Lord,' will enter the kingdom of
> heaven, but only he who does the will of my Father who is
> in heaven. Many will say to me on that day, 'Lord, Lord,
> did we not prophesy in your name, and in your name
> drive out demons and perform many miracles?' Then I will
> tell them plainly, 'I never knew you. Away from me, you
> evildoers!'
>
> *Matthew 7:20–23*

It is only the people who are travelling the road of blessing who enter the state of bliss: not because of divine favouritism, but because only the road of blessing goes that way. That's how it is.

Jesus says, 'I am the Way, the Truth and the Life: no one comes to the Father but by me' (John 14:6, my paraphrase). It is the cross of Jesus that holds all things together, that sits at the heart of creation.

The cross is a tree of death and a tree of life. Every tree

puts forth roots into the dark earth and branches into the light air, and is an agent of transformation, balancing carbon dioxide with oxygen, and managing the passage of life-giving water through the earth and the air. This balancing and transformative role of trees is essential and life-giving. Without it, there is chaos – the earth begins to suffer conditions of extreme (drought and flood); and the layer in which new life can start is eroded and swept away by the wild elements of water and wind. Jesus, you remember, said to the wind and the water in their wildness, 'Peace, be still' (Mark 4:39 KJV): he is the creator of stability (peace and contentment). Trees create stability too.

The cross of Jesus, tree of life and tree of death, is the place where endings are transformed into beginnings. Jesus passed through life into death, and through death into life. God created in him a touchstone of transformation. He became the Alpha and the Omega. In him we can find rest for our weariness – the end of striving; but also new energy, the beginning of life and hope.

The tree is a crossing place: both in nature, and in the tree of life and death that is the cross.

To know Jesus and walk in his way, to enter the crossing place at the heart of life and death, beginnings and endings, is to step into life, to realize peace and contentment, to travel the road of blessing.

Jesus is some*one*, not some*thing*. To know Jesus is to enter a relationship, not crack a code or create a formula. Therefore the Truth that Jesus is, is a truth that we get to know, become acquainted with personally: not a head-knowledge or a doctrine, but a friendship. We know Jesus only by travelling with him. And the Way that Jesus is, is a way of *being*, a journey – not 'this is the way you do it', a prescriptive set of rules and dogmas. The Life that Jesus is, is the life you live – habit, dailiness – not a prize.

So, some people have started on the road of blessing who don't know they know Jesus – like the disciples enthusiastically casting out demons and healing the sick when they didn't even know how to pray. Everyone following the road of blessing will eventually know they know Jesus – enlightenment will come one day: 'Oh, *right*! It was *you*!' Of course they will: because Jesus *is* the Way. But they might not know at first – because you can join the road of blessing at any point, and only gradually does it unfold under your feet. You know what your feet are, don't you? They are your self-understanding.

There has been a lot to take in, in this chapter. Let me recap the basic points for you:

1. God exists.
2. God created everything.
3. The *ruach* (wind/spirit/breath) of God in creation is the life force that animates everything, giving it meaning and making it more than just stuff.
4. Human beings, the children of 'Earthy' and 'Life', bear the image of God, and are designed to follow in his way – to move with the flow of his Spirit.
5. The flow of the Spirit is the road of blessing.
6. To travel in the road of blessing brings you into relationship with Jesus, but you might not be conscious of that at first.
7. The road of blessing creates an experiential connection with the transformative power of the tree of life and death (the cross of Jesus) that sits at the heart of creation, facilitating both transformation and stability in the

changing fortunes of our lives, which are the gift of God (Isaiah 45:7).

8. You can join the road of blessing at any point, just as you are; there is no procedural order or prerequisite.

9. It is very important to make a start, because one of the strongest things in life is habit; and to form a habit, you do have to begin.

10. The seed of going badly pear-shaped is inherent in every life that is not following the road of blessing.

Chapter Two

How Do We Recognize the Road
of Blessing?

In Chapter One, we looked at the first principle of the road of blessing: that there is a pattern to life; it is not random. It has a directional flow, moving with the current of the will of God, which is always towards justice, faithfulness, mercy, truth, peace, wisdom, kindness, healing, gentleness, love, understanding, goodness and humility.

Let's assume we are keen to begin, ready to make a start – so where is the road of blessing, and how do we get on it? How can we tell in making choices which decisions might take us with the flow of God's will, and which might set us off in the wrong direction? We know that learning to be wise and good will involve struggle, requiring effort and prayer – so how do we know the difference between the struggle that is building our character and the struggle that is because we are going against the flow?

A friend of mine who had just been through a bad week said to me: 'The old Devil's really been attacking me this week – unless it's the Lord trying to tell me something!' I found that striking, because she had been a born-again, baptized-in-the-Spirit Christian for more than fifty years, and still couldn't tell the difference between the forces of good and the forces of evil – and she was a thinking, intelligent woman with a very analytical mind, steeped in prayer. What chances have the rest of us got?

I saw a little squirrel once, which was very inadvisedly trying to cross a dual carriageway. Speed limit 70 miles per hour, very heavy traffic. The squirrel had made it across the first lane, and was just having second thoughts as the cars raced by. It had paused, and lifted its tiny hand to its mouth in doubtful hesitation: 'Ermm… oh 'eck!'

We need not kid ourselves that we are often as vulnerable as the squirrel, but it's true enough that we often share the same sense of total overload: 'I actually do not feel able to do this.' So, how do we find the way?

We have several guideposts: Scripture, the faith community and its faith tradition, observation, nature, conscience and direct leading accessed through prayer. These act as checks and balances against each other, which is important, as none alone will give us the complete picture. So, Scripture is holy and God-breathed, but if our interpretation of it is anti-nature, or divisive and destructive in the faith community, and our choices and behaviour are ruining people's lives, then we need to rethink our interpretation. Or if our conscience tells us something is perfectly okay but Scripture says it is not, and observation shows that what we are doing is blessing no one, we might conclude our conscience needs a little updating.

Scripture

In this book you will notice that I draw often on the Bible for authority and insight.

In the coronation service of the Church of England, the new monarch is presented with a Bible, with these words: 'we present you with this Book, the most valuable thing that this world affords. Here is Wisdom; this is the royal Law; these are the lively Oracles of God.'

The Methodist Church teaches that the Bible was inspired by God and contains all things necessary for salvation, so that when it is read and studied under the inspiration of the Holy Spirit, we can have confidence in it as our true rule and guide for both faith and practice – not that the Methodist Church above every other should have the last word on the matter, but I do believe their statement of faith about the Bible creates an affirmation almost all Christians could sign their names to.

The Bible is immensely important to following the road of blessing, because it is our map. It shows us where we've come from, shows the road we've travelled, helps us to locate the sacred hot spots where we touch the life of God, and shows us which way to go.

Some people get onto the road of blessing without having read the Bible, because we don't have to do things in order: but to follow the road of blessing all the way to its conclusion, your life would have to be illuminated by the wisdom of the Scriptures.

If we ask Bible-believing Christians *why* you have to respect its teaching, they will often point us to 2 Timothy 3:16: 'All Scripture is God-breathed and is useful for teaching, rebuking, correcting and training in righteousness.' To simply point to this text is unsatisfactory, for you are then operating a circular argument – you must accept the authority of the Bible because the Bible says you should – which still doesn't explain what gives the Bible its authority in the first place.

To understand *that*, we are helped by one of our other guide-posts: observation. We can observe that the documents forming the Bible have arisen from lives of profound faith. The experiences of such visionaries as Abraham and Moses are written here. The life and teaching of Jesus of Nazareth plays out before us here. The struggle and learning and pilgrimage of a huge body of people of faith are represented here. These are not the writings of a learned professor who has formulated a worldview; this is much bigger and older and wider and deeper than that. It records for us, with real honesty, leaving out nothing of the failure, weakness and sin, how this great faith community experienced the presence of God. And in some places the writings in it claim to be direct revelation.

So we can observe that it encompasses messages and experiences of tremendous spiritual power. Our observation doesn't have to stop there, though: some have called the Bible 'a living book', meaning that, in an extraordinary way, it meets each one of us where we are, addressing our fears and uncertainties, our questions and longings, bringing peace and confidence and faith. It has about it a quality of the miraculous. Reading and studying the Bible changes people – that is not my opinion only, it is observable, recorded fact. A person would have to be either completely obtuse or determinedly antagonistic to evaluate the Bible as an ordinary or unimportant set of books.

I would say then, don't be browbeaten by others, or accept the doctrines of the already converted, or feel pressurized by a sense of majority opinion – taste and see. Read it. Try it. Explore it. Work with it.

The authority of the Bible and its place in the life of a disciple is the cause of much dissension, and at the root of many bitter schisms and even hatred. That this is the case is more than ironic, it is shameful; for this is the Book of Love, the book that asks us to go out of our way to understand, encourage, respect, reconcile and forgive. Any who allow the Bible to be a cause of schism have invalidated their own cause – for the Bible records the fervent prayer of Jesus (John 17:20–21): 'I pray also for those who will believe in me... that all of them may be one.' It was not the teaching of Jesus that doctrinal purity should take precedence over unity – quite the reverse. In his life, teaching and example, he showed us that we should bear with imperfection for the sake of unity and love.

For instance, he appointed Judas, the thief, to be his treasurer; the whole group therefore carrying the consequences of this character flaw, rather than expelling Judas to deal with it on his own. This was because of love; because trust and patience heal people.

Jesus was not afraid of the imperfection of others. When he embraced the leper, instead of Jesus catching leprosy, the leper caught a little bit of what Jesus had, and went away healed. This is how he asks us to live.

In accepting the Bible as our rule and guide, we are not called to be harshly inquisitorial about how others relate to that sacred text. We are called, according to our light, to respond to it in holiness of life: that's all.

There is a way of reading the Bible that allows us to live under the rule of its authority without schism or fragmenting into factions. This is very important to grasp, if our purpose in getting acquainted with the Scriptures is to advance us along the road of blessing.

Following the road of blessing absolutely requires of us a peaceable spirit – an attitude of gentleness and humility (more about that later on). So if we accept the authority of the Bible to help us along the road of blessing, then allow ourselves to be drawn into antagonism and schism over its place in our lives – well, we've just shot ourselves in the foot, haven't we?

This is the key – we have to stay *inside the text*. As soon as I say the Bible is this or that – 'the Bible is divinely inspired', 'the Bible is literally true from cover to cover', 'the Bible is the Word of God' – then I have stepped out of the text into my own opinion: I have made myself the arbiter and judge of what the Bible is and how we should all relate to it. As soon as I have decreed what the Bible is and how it is to be used, I have set myself above it – overruled everyone else with my own opinion and interpretation. But if I am content to stay inside the text – not to start making pronouncements about what this is and what we've all got to do about it, but just let it go to work on my soul, change me, teach me, inspire me, transform me – then it remains effective as my rule and guide in following the road of blessing.

When I read the Bible and am challenged to discover that it says: 'Wives, submit to your husbands as to the Lord' (Ephesians 5:22), instead of setting myself up as judge over it – saying either: 'That's right!' or 'That's ridiculous!' – I can choose to stay inside the text, allowing it to interact with me and illuminate me, exploring what wisdom it may have, permitting it to challenge my preconceptions and assumptions. If I react by stepping out of the text – thinking: 'Hmm. Mrs Collins at chapel could do with a little Ephesians 5:22 ministry!' or 'Christianity is a patriarchal religion and this is but one of many examples of the subjugation of women in its tradition' – then I have also stepped out of the way of blessing, and made myself a judge over others.

Whether I am right or not isn't the issue. People join the way of blessing where and how they are; and similarly, the Bible meets and interacts with people as they are at the moment. The light this verse sheds on my life today may be different from the light it sheds in fifteen years' time; and different from the light it sheds on Mrs Collins' path, or on the preacher's or the pastor's path.

If the Bible is a map for the way of blessing, it will show me where I am, and where next to set my feet: but I have no idea where the other people are, so I can't tell which way the Bible will be showing them to go.

If I stay within the text, I will stay on the road of blessing: and I can trust the Bible to help me find my way.

The faith community and its faith tradition

We sent Timothy, who is our brother and God's fellow worker in spreading the gospel of Christ, to strengthen and encourage you in your faith, so that no one would be unsettled by these trials.

1 Thessalonians 3:2–3

We have come to this world to hold our light steady through all the turbulence and perplexities of physical existence. We have come to find the secret of happiness that endures even in the midst of suffering and trouble. Following the road of blessing means achieving that kind of inner stability: a faith which is really established, shining calmly and steadily.

There are those in the faith community, and there is wisdom in the faith tradition, that can help us find the way to such a faith and such a light. We have to have our eyes open here, to discern wisely.

The faith tradition is very old. Many hundreds of years have passed since the church began. As time has gone on, visions have settled into customs, and these have sometimes retained their life, but sometimes become a hindrance, accretions gathered over time that become ends in themselves and distract us from the journey we came here to make.

The faith community is a source of great light and compassion. Through contact with the household of faith, people find healing and peace. It takes little reflection to understand that, such being the case, at any given time the faith community will have many tired, fragile and unstable souls on board.

I was once sent to preach at the evening worship of a small-town chapel. The lectionary readings set for the day were all about resurrection. I came down from the preacher's desk to talk with the people, asking them 'What experiences of resurrection have happened to you in your own life? What times can you think of, when you felt lost and hopeless, but surprising new possibilities came out of those difficult times?'

This congregation was well used to me asking them real questions and expecting real answers, but on this occasion, nobody responded. I knew them well: knew that some were carrying heartaches, struggling with illness and bereavement. None of them responded to me.

I asked a little more, and those who had anything to say told me that they were even now in hopelessness: they could see no light.

I asked them what they found in chapel to raise them up and help them – asked them why they continued in such difficult circumstances to come to chapel.

Out of the slow, sad, bewildered silence, eventually a woman in turn asked of me: 'Well – where else should we go?'

It reminded me of Jesus, asking his disciples during a time

of great resistance to his ministry, 'Will you also go away?'; and Peter responding, 'Lord, to whom should we go?' (John 6:68, my paraphrase). Even when the way seems to go nowhere, Jesus is still the Way. Even when everything is baffling, Jesus is still the Truth. Even when everything is slipping away from us, he is the Life, abundant Life.

People go through some rough times, and part of what will be asked of us as we make this journey is to share some of our light and love and happiness with them, to encourage them and lift them up. But to make the journey, we ourselves will also need encouragement – and in the faith community only some, not all, of the souls we encounter will understand about the road of blessing, or be able to help us find it.

So in seeking the wisdom of the tradition and the encouragement of the faithful, we may have to pick our way carefully. It's like digging potatoes for supper: that patch of the vegetable garden will certainly reward our seeking – but we may have to dig about a bit and be prepared to shake loose a fair bit of clinging compost, before we have what we were looking for.

Even so, the faith community and tradition are repositories of power and wisdom. As we begin to study the Bible and engage with its texts, it will help us immensely to be taken deeper into that treasure store by the learning of scholars who understand the historical and cultural resonances, the Hebrew and the Greek. As we learn the skills and art of holding our light steady, it makes all the difference to be travelling along with companions in the faith, spiritual kindred who can remind us of our vision, pray for us, and respond to our failures and disappointments with grace and understanding.

We also build up an amazing vibration for healing and

transformation when we come together in prayer and praise, immersing ourselves as a group in the power of the Holy Spirit, singing or chanting or praying, lifting one another into the light.

I went to stay one blustery October on the beautiful island of Iona off the coast of Scotland. In the Abbey community one evening while I was there, we shared in a service of light. At the end of it, for the symbolism, we each were given a lighted candle to carry out into the dark night beyond the safe walls of the chapel. Every single person's light blew out the minute they crossed the threshold!

Now, I found this very amusing, especially as it was not far from my observations from my life back at home. In church, we sang praises and prayed sincerely: but as soon as we got out of the building, many of us went back to living much of our lives as if all that we had prayed and read and sung were only fairy stories.

Watch and pray. When you come to the faith community, look for the people who are holding their light steady beyond the walls of the chapel: the people who remain cheerful and serene even in redundancy, illness, bereavement; the people who share with others even when they have little themselves; the people who are generous and forgiving towards others, who are kind as well as honest in business, who handle money with integrity; who make choices with a thought for social justice and the well-being of creation. Not everyone in the faith community will be shining so steady – but some will, and those are the ones who will help and encourage you on the road of blessing.

In the faith tradition, some aspects will speak to your condition while others leave you cold. When I go to choral evensong at a great cathedral, the peaceful, leisurely chanting of the psalms always gives my soul the space it needs to reflect upon and be challenged by the wisdom in the holy Word. The huge, ancient building, mounting up into mystery, refreshes me and centres me again: it seems to be drenched in holiness, full of kindness and the slow, deep, solemn joy of the Way. But I know well that there are some among my friends I would never invite to accompany me – who are driven crazy by 'all that droning', who find nothing but archaic dust and empty ceremony in cathedral worship. We are all different, and bring our variety into the road of blessing: but *somewhere* in the tradition, you will find the springs of grace, touch the living heartbeat – and it is well worth the trouble of looking.

Observation

Learning how to look, and learning to trust what you see, plays a large part in discovering the road of blessing and gaining confidence in following it.

It is necessary to get this the right way round: when we follow the road of blessing, we are looking out for what we know will be there, on the track of the signs of the invisible reality that determines everything else – knowing, as Jesus put it, how to read the signs of the times (Matthew 16:1–3). So we are establishing our vision first of all; and then our vision will be the lens we look through. It is very important that we work this way round: if we do things the other way, and allow the appearance of circumstances to buffet us around, we shall quickly become discouraged, and likely to give up.

Job had this trouble, gazing around himself in disbelief at all his calamities, asking in bewilderment: 'Why do the wicked live on, growing old and increasing in power? They see their children established around them, their offspring before their eyes. Their homes are safe and free from fear; the rod of God is not upon them' (Job 21:7–9). But the book of Job encourages us to take the longer view – to read to the end of the story.

I love the *Book of Common Prayer* translation of Psalm 9:18: 'For the poor shall not alway be forgotten: the patient abiding of the meek shall not perish for ever.'

When all seems lost, it is because we cannot see what is to come. This is true even in the most extreme circumstances. We have a phrase in the preaching tradition of the church: 'the foot of the cross', saying that all the best preachers bring their hearers to the this place. I wonder how the first people at the foot of the cross felt? Numbed in disbelief; beside themselves with horror and pity and a sense of betrayal as they watched Jesus die; terrified and distraught? They must have thought it was all over, that their dreams were shattered and all they had pinned their faith on was lost. They could not have imagined that two thousand years on, we should be encouraging all preachers to bring their hearers to the foot of the cross – and thinking of that as a *good* thing!

Developing this discipline of seeing does not come easily to us. My children's father, a musician and a free spirit, operated by a timetable entirely his own. When he left the house, I never knew when I might see him again. He could leave calling cheerily that he was just popping down to get fuel for the car – and not come back for two hours. I have whiled away a significant portion of my life waiting patiently on the corner by the supermarket, surrounded with bags of shopping and wondering where on earth he could have got to this time. Several times, I concluded that the worst had happened and he had met with a dreadful accident. Standing by the road huddled against the wind, I mentally reviewed our budget and prospects, considered how I would cope with raising our children alone, thought about who he would have liked to play the organ at his funeral – and then over the hill our battered old Volvo would roll into view…

In the same way, the people of God have sometimes looked around them and concluded: 'No, really. He must have forgotten us. Either God is dead, or he never existed, or he hates us or he simply doesn't care.' As the psalmist says: 'But as for me, my feet had almost slipped; I had nearly lost my foothold. For I envied the arrogant when I saw the prosperity of the wicked' (Psalm 73:2–3).

So, taking the road of blessing involves a certain adjustment of our vision: 'Now faith is being sure of what we hope for and certain of what we do not see' (Hebrews 11:1); 'We live by faith, not by sight' (2 Corinthians 5:7).

This is not the same as being gullible and unrealistic: it is a matter of understanding the law of cause and effect that governs the universe, and the direction of flow in the act of creation.

In creating, spirit comes first, and matter flows from it. The first great Cause is God, who is Spirit: without him, nothing would exist. Without the creative urge of God's Spirit, there would be no physical universe. This sets a precedent we can trust. What originates in our spirit will sooner or later show up in our physical world. Our attitudes and thoughts and beliefs will determine our daily experience, and go to work upon the circumstances we encounter to shape and modify them. As Paul succinctly expresses it in Galatians 6:7: 'Do not be deceived: God cannot be mocked. A man reaps what he sows.'

This is the law of cause and effect, and it can be trusted. There are two aspects of it that we need to have a firm handle on: the first is that the flow is *from* spirit *to* matter – the road of blessing operates by our thoughts determining our circumstances, *not the other way round*. The second is that everything we do, say or think is a cause which will create an effect – as we sow, so shall we reap; this is biblical principle.

Patience comes into this, and so does insight. The effects we cause are not always immediately apparent, and not always apparent at all to ourselves. My family likes to refer to 'the red car on the motorway' phenomenon, ever since we saw an extraordinary piece of film footage on a television programme about traffic policing. The film showed a bright-red car coming roaring down a slip road into heavy and fast-moving traffic on a motorway. Without even pausing, the driver tore down at speed into the traffic, and proceeded to weave his way through, dodging from lane to lane. Astonishingly, he did not collide with anyone, and must have driven away imagining he had not caused any problems at all – 'Got away with that one!'

But the camera picked up the scene of devastation he left behind him. Distracting and disconcerting other drivers as he went, he left a trail of mayhem – not one accident, but a whole series.

I believe that what we put into this world will eventually manifest in our own lives, because we are not separate from everything and everyone else – we are one but not-one. But even while we are waiting for that to happen, the causes we create may manifest as effects in our environment: we create the circumstances that are either creative or destructive in the lives of others, whether we mean to, whether we notice, or not.

The effects of the causes we have set in motion may not immediately be apparent. Between the time of my writing this and the time of your reading it, I expect to have become a grandmother. Chatting on the telephone to my daughter late on in her pregnancy, it occurred to me how terrifying and bewildering it would be to be pregnant if you didn't know what pregnancy was. 'I think you'd figure it out,' said my daughter: 'I think at least you'd be able to work out you had some kind of living creature in there – though you might well wonder how on earth it would get out, or if it would continue to grow until it filled you up completely!'

The rhythm of cause and effect in our lives is the same as sowing seeds that grow into flowers and vegetables, or implanting the seed that grows into a baby. There is uncertainty. There is a time lapse. Of course, not every act of intercourse results in a baby, and personally I have never had any luck with carrot seed in the garden either. I'm not saying the law of cause and effect is that simplistic: what I'm saying is, there can be a time delay between the intention, the focus, the thought that arises in your spirit, and the manifestation of that thought in the circumstances of your life. But the process in general can be trusted – not every couple makes a baby every time, but this is how babies are made.

In similar wise, what we put our attention on, we get more of; what we think about increases; what we focus on will multiply – and even when the connections are not clear to us, everything we do, say or think makes a difference. As Jesus said: 'Make a tree good and its fruit will be good, or make a tree bad and its fruit will be bad, for a tree is recognized by its fruit' (Matthew 12:33); the process starts with the thoughts and attitudes that we bear on the inside, and these will effect and affect the developing circumstances of our lives.

If we want to follow the road of blessing, we must grasp this principle, and start to notice it. People who don't notice things don't learn. I met a man in his sixties dying of lung cancer in a hospice, who told me: 'They say that it's smoking gives you lung cancer, but it isn't true – I know, because I've smoked all my life.' The principle of cause and effect, even when it is right under your nose, can be overlooked: we have to develop a seeing eye.

Once we know what we're looking for – once we grasp that what we see does not shape our belief, rather what we believe shapes what we eventually see – we begin to notice the law of cause and effect in operation. We learn not to trust in circumstances, but to deepen our faith and prayer to bring about the circumstances we would like to see. We notice that as we think and speak and act in the flow of God's loving purpose, all things begin to work together for our good: 'Do not conform any longer to the pattern of this world, but be transformed by the renewing of your mind. Then you will be able to test and approve what God's will is – his good, pleasing and perfect will' (Romans 12:2).

The biblical principle is to begin with our vision – to allow our insight to determine our sight; to let what we believe set the agenda for what we will see:

> Against all hope, Abraham in hope believed and so became
> the father of many nations, just as it had been said to
> him, 'So shall your offspring be.' Without weakening
> in his faith, he faced the fact that his body was as good
> as dead – since he was about a hundred years old – and
> that Sarah's womb was also dead. Yet he did not waver
> through unbelief regarding the promise of God, but was

strengthened in his faith and gave glory to God, being
fully persuaded that God had power to do what he had
promised.

Romans 4:18–21

Jesus urges us to use our powers of observation, to look beyond
appearances, letting our understanding of the law of cause and
effect make us intelligent to discern what is before us:

Watch out for false prophets. They come to you in sheep's
clothing, but inwardly they are ferocious wolves. By their
fruit you will recognize them. Do people pick grapes from
thornbushes, or figs from thistles? Likewise every good tree
bears good fruit, but a bad tree bears bad fruit. A good tree
cannot bear bad fruit, and a bad tree cannot bear good
fruit.

Matthew 7:15–18

He is saying that, like the red car on the motorway, you can
see what kind of a driver has passed this way; you can see what
sort of cause they are instigating in their thoughts and attitude,
by the effect they have. It's important to look deeply; some
people are troublemakers because they have dissentious spirits
and confrontational attitudes, whereas others stir up trouble
because they speak with a prophet's voice to a complacent
and decadent community. In our looking and weighing and
discerning, we need to be immersing ourselves in prayer, and
also walking in the discipline of faith ourselves; this sharpens
our perception.

It is important to understand that this is not the same
as saying, 'Get saved and everything will be hunky-dory after
that.' To be justified – rightly aligned with God's will – is not a

43

guarantee of an easy ride; quite the opposite, if anything. John Wimber joked in typical style in a sermon: 'Get filled with the Holy Spirit, and spend the rest of your life desperate!'

This law of cause and effect is not about creating a broad and flowery path to bliss, but about knowing how to transform our experience of life within the context of our circumstances, whatever they may be. My mother once remarked to my sister, 'I don't know how Pen does it – I think she must have a private income!' I didn't: my budget never did work on paper; but I was following the road of blessing, so somehow my bills always got paid.

Paul writes in several places about this transformation of experience by following the road of blessing:

> Rejoice in the Lord always. I will say it again: Rejoice! Let your gentleness be evident to all. The Lord is near. Do not be anxious about anything, but in everything, by prayer and petition, with thanksgiving, present your requests to God. And the peace of God, which transcends all understanding, will guard your hearts and your minds in Christ Jesus.
>
> Finally, brothers, whatever is true, whatever is noble, whatever is right, whatever is pure, whatever is lovely, whatever is admirable – if anything is excellent or praiseworthy – think about such things. Whatever you have learned or received or heard from me, or seen in me – put it into practice. And the God of peace will be with you.
>
> … I have learned to be content whatever the circumstances. I know what it is to be in need, and I know what it is to have plenty. I have learned the secret of being content in any and every situation, whether well fed

or hungry, whether living in plenty or in want. I can do everything through him who gives me strength.

Philippians 4:4–9, 11b–13

We must grasp that this is not poetic waffle – he means what he is saying. It is practical, useful, and can be tested in our own daily experience.

In 2 Corinthians 6:10, Paul describes himself and his companions as 'sorrowful, yet always rejoicing; poor, yet making many rich; having nothing, and yet possessing everything.' The New English Bible translates that last phrase as 'penniless, we own the world', which for me sums up the freedom, light-heartedness and joy to be found in following the road of blessing.

Once we begin to live this way, people are often eager to explain to us that it can't be done, or point out in triumph the apparent flaws in the proposition. They remind us of people who believed in the power of healing prayer, who were prayed for in faith, but died anyway. They remind us of people of faith who were made redundant, who got horrible illnesses, whose lives were fragmented by dreadful tragedies. They are failing to grasp that it isn't that we need to get on the road of blessing so that bad things don't happen to us – it's that we need to be on the road of blessing because bad things most certainly *will* happen to us. It's in times of sorrow and hardship that we most rely on and appreciate the road of blessing. As Psalm 84:5–6 expresses it: 'Blessed are those whose strength is in you, who have set their hearts on pilgrimage. As they pass through the Valley of Baca [Vale of Tears], they make it a place of springs.'

During the time I worked in a hospice, a patient came in who was visited on several occasions by a lady with a healing ministry, who prayed for the sick woman and laid hands on her. Some of the staff responded with scepticism, seeing that the patient still deteriorated and eventually died: others were intrigued to see that though the patient died, her last days were full of peace, calm and dignity – light shone within her.

One of our guideposts to the road of blessing is observation: 'What I say unto you, I say unto all: Watch' (Mark 13:37 KJV). Finding our way to the road of blessing requires us to keep our eyes open: not to believe everything we are told, or accept pre-packaged ideologies. We have to learn from experience, and we learn by looking and reflecting – but we do have to understand what we're looking at, and what we're looking for.

Nature

I have puzzled for a long time about the role of what we call 'Nature', in helping us find our feet on the road of blessing. It seems to me that there are two principal ideological pitfalls in contemplating 'Nature'. Some people make the mistake of worshipping and sentimentalizing nature, not making the important step of discovering the hand of the creator in creation. We are called to 'fill the earth and subdue it'. I like to think of that not as overrunning and dominating the earth, but as bringing out the best in it and (in such disciplines as science, medicine, geology, economics, agriculture and education) engaging with Christ's ministry of reconciliation to help living systems flow in harmony for the well-being of all creation.

It may seem arrogant to suggest that we should be able to help living systems flow in harmony: as we acquaint ourselves with the warp and woof of ecology and the environment, we have to marvel at the delicate and interwoven complexity of eco-systems and wilderness – the pattern of divine creating, which we unbalance at our peril. Yet it takes not too much reflection to see that we can work with what God has made to help and to heal – we do have a contribution to make. The Indian Ocean Tsunami of 2004 provides a good instance of the role human beings can play: together we can use our skills in medicine, engineering, organization and food production (among many others) to bring healing and peace in places where the wildness of nature has brought injury, terror and trauma to the communities of our own kind.

It is when we work against nature, consuming too much too quickly, destabilizing the natural ecology of the earth and giving no time or space for regeneration, that we tear and destroy the fabric of life – of which we are a part, our own well-being inextricably involved with that which we are blindly destroying. And this is the other ideological pitfall: thinking ourselves separate from nature, as though the living world were no more than a resource for our consumption.

God, who is love, factors in love wherever he creates. In delivering the earth into our governance, we can take it for granted that he has expected we will cherish the earth, steward and nurture and respect the earth, treat it with love: for that is God's way. It is the road of blessing – God does nothing in any other way, and asks no less of us in acting as his ordained representatives.

That God has delivered the earth into our governance is plainly true: it is a biblical reality and a matter of faith, but it is also an observable reality on the most mundane of levels. Our species and ours alone is set fair to wreck and destroy the entire planet with all its wonder and beauty, the balance of life, by a fatal combination of ignorance and selfishness. The responsibility belongs to us, whatever our religious beliefs: the truth that starts in the spirit manifests in due course in the physical realm, and so it is with the stewardship of the earth and the consequences of our sin in that context.

God's creation is one living web. When a modern car breaks down, the faulty unit can be identified and replaced, a new unit patched in. But God's creation is holistic: our place within it is part of an unbroken continuum. The Bible story expresses this in telling of the Fall of humankind, in which the human breaking of faith with God cannot be isolated to the one species; it has affected the whole of creation by introducing death into life. So the healing must also be holistic:

> The creation waits in eager expectation for the sons of
> God to be revealed. For the creation was subjected to
> frustration, not by its own choice, but by the will of the
> one who subjected it, in hope that the creation itself will
> be liberated from its bondage to decay and brought into
> the glorious freedom of the children of God.
>
> *Romans 8:19–21*

We are not-one but one: the sin that we have brought into the world has spread through everything, so that creation groans and struggles, travailing to bring to birth the order of God's peaceable Kingdom. When we align ourselves upon the pattern of God's grace, healing will flow through us into all creation, bringing the beautiful freedom of grace to restore and renew what has been lost and tarnished and broken.

Actually to follow the road of blessing means finding a wise balance between respecting natural systems, and discovering the proper role and contribution for us to make in fulfilling our God-ordained human responsibility. It means accepting our creation ordinance as stewards of the earth, and being willing to live redeemed lives that will draw the whole web of creation into redemption.

But for the moment we are thinking about how 'Nature', creation, helps us to establish our feet in the way of blessing in the first place. It starts with understanding that everything has a point of view; this is a key concept in finding our way into the road of blessing, so that we are working with the flow of life and not against it.

As a gardener, my husband is at war with slugs and snails from the deepest and most visceral level. And he has a point of view: if he plants out a tray of lettuces and the slugs demolish the lot over night, we shall go hungry. The lettuces have a point of view too – they have a right to their time in the sun, there is a place that is theirs in the world, and my husband protects and champions their point of view. But, slugs and snails also have a point of view. They are part of the service industry of the earth's ecosystem, helping with the essential task of decomposition, recycling leaves and faeces and anything else lying around, returning to the earth the nutrients locked up in organic matter. Slugs and snails replenish the fertility of the earth, and so contribute to the well-being of both plants and humans.

Songbirds have a point of view too. They like to eat snails – our garden is full of empty snail shells that blackbirds have left behind (I use these for the drainage layer at the bottom of plant pots). Metaldehyde slug bait can be eaten by songbirds in mistake for food, and will of course poison the snails that feed the blackbirds as well as poisoning slugs.

Lapwings and skylarks have greatly declined in numbers

with modern farming methods, and both dunnocks and meadow pipits are almost halved in numbers. Climate change, denaturing of the environment and pesticide treatments have probably contributed greatly to their decline. As they have declined and climate change has threatened the survival of migrating birds' seasonal patterns, the cuckoo, herald of the English spring, is vanishing. Climate change has also brought drought to the African winter home of the cuckoo.

When we adopt wildlife-friendly gardening and farming practices, the meadow pipit nesting on the moorland and heath, and the dunnock nesting in woods and gardens, may begin to return – and so provide unwitting hospitality to the cuckoo. And in making bird-friendly gardens and farms, planting trees and hedgerows, thinking up ways to protect crops against pests and disease without threatening other species, we would also protect the earth for ourselves. Trees and all plants slow down the movement of water through landscape, protecting our homes against drought and flood.

When we remember the point of view of the slug... the snail... the songbird... the migrating bird... the moth... the beetle... the tree... we find that we have taken care of the point of view of the human: we have found our way into the road of blessing.

The intricacy, beauty and complexity of the earth also awaken our souls to God. Even when our intellects understand about biological processes and chemical reactions, our souls still look upon the birth of a lamb, the emergence of the lotus from the swamp, the dance of starlings at dusk, the pageant of glory in the sunrise, the wonder of falling in love – and see a miracle.

When we work with what is natural, we walk in blessing;

and so nature is our teacher and our guide. When we think holistically, as best we can integrating the point of view of all living things, we find ourselves surprised by blessing at every turn.

Sometimes, remembering the point of view of other creatures means accepting limitations. If, having stripped out the oil from the earth's veins until we can no longer fuel our aeroplanes, instead of razing the last of the rainforest to plant palm groves and taking the food of the poor to fuel machines, we simply *accept less*, for the sake of the point of view of the poor and the point of view of every living thing that shares this earth with us – then we shall fulfil our creation ordinance, and we shall enter the road of blessing.

It helps us to recognize that, as we are one but not-one, for each of us the road of blessing will be a unique path. We are travelling together, we are moving in the flow of God's will, but our footprints will be our very own.

So it is that for some, remembering the point of view of other species may mean embracing a vegan way of life. Raising meat, eggs, cheese and dairy products requires heavy consumption of oil and grain, often involves terrible cruelty and sensory deprivation for the animals, and always implies very premature death – the death of male chicks so that females alone grow up to lay eggs, the death of calves so that the milk produced by their mothers may be taken for dairy produce. For some people, once they begin to look more deeply into the point of view of other creatures than themselves, this is simply unacceptable. For the sake of compassion, they withdraw from it, and this leads them into the road of blessing.

Others, as they think about how the food on their plate got there, may respond differently. They feel the relationship between humans and agricultural animals is a privilege, a wonderful thing. They treasure the gentle presence of cows and pigs and sheep – their hearts lift at the sight of the spring lambs or a mother hen gathering her chicks. They accept the agricultural cycle of birth and death as a part of the natural way of things, seeing well-managed slaughter as preferable to death in the wild under the claws and teeth of a predator, and the year a lamb lives in a humanely run farm as better than no chance of life at all. So for the sake of compassion, they take the trouble to source their victuals from farmers who treat the earth kindly, remembering the point of view of wildlife, working with the rhythms and heartbeat of the land, husbanding gently their beasts and leaving enough space for wilderness. And this choice, too, can lead us into the road of blessing: it's not so much the detail of specific practice as the wisdom and compassion that motivate it that makes the difference.

When we walk lightly on the earth, we walk in blessing: as individuals, as communities, as a species.

According to the Bible, nature is orientated towards God: we can read about this especially in the book of Job and the book of Psalms. The Bible sees living creatures of all species as looking towards God, as having their eyes fixed upon God, both in adoration and in reliance upon divine providence. If we too learn to live like that – lives of trust and praise, wholly and consciously reliant upon God – then we shall be following in the way of blessing.

There is an interesting passage in Luke's gospel that alludes to the orientation of nature towards the purposes of God:

> When he [Jesus] came near the place where the road goes
> down the Mount of Olives, the whole crowd of disciples
> began joyfully to praise God in loud voices for all the
> miracles they had seen:
>
> 'Blessed is the king who comes in the name of the
> Lord!'
>
> 'Peace in heaven and glory in the highest!'
>
> Some of the Pharisees in the crowd said to Jesus,
> 'Teacher, rebuke your disciples!'
>
> 'I tell you,' he replied, 'if they keep quiet, the stones
> will cry out.'
>
> *Luke 19:37–40*

We cannot be clear whether Jesus meant this literally or
figuratively – whether he meant that the stones would have
physically sung, or whether he simply meant that for his
disciples to be silenced would avail nothing, because all
creation witnesses to divine truth and adores God's glory and
responds to God's presence. Either way, what we can be clear
about is that nature is God-orientated: so if we stay close to
what is natural and beneficial to the earth, we shall be moving
in the way of blessing.

Conscience

Our conscience is designed to lead us into the road of blessing
– that's what it's for:

> And if the Spirit of him who raised Jesus from the dead
> is living in you, he who raised Christ from the dead will
> also give life to your mortal bodies through his Spirit, who
> lives in you.

> Therefore, brothers, we have an obligation – but it is
> not to the sinful nature, to live according to it. For if you
> live according to the sinful nature, you will die; but if
> by the Spirit you put to death the misdeeds of the body,
> you will live, because those who are led by the Spirit of
> God are sons of God. For you did not receive a spirit that
> makes you a slave again to fear, but you received the Spirit
> of sonship. And by him we cry, '*Abba*, Father.' The Spirit
> himself testifies with our spirit that we are God's children.
>
> *Romans 8:11–16*

The King James Version renders verse 16: 'The Spirit itself beareth witness with our spirit, that we are the children of God.'

The letter to the Romans is very useful in helping us to understand how our conscience directs us toward the road of blessing. Paul acknowledges that we can be double-minded, pulled off course by anger or selfishness or self-importance.

Any day of the week you can meet people whose religion is basically about themselves: there is 'me', and then there is 'everything else', and when it comes to a choice, 'me' comes first. This makes such people very unsteady and unbalanced as they try to walk in faith: because every time something happens that feels uncomfortable or disadvantageous to 'me', they are knocked off course.

This is how you get people who can be in a big celebration singing all about self on the cross and Christ on the throne – 'Jesus, Jesus I surrender all my life to you' – and then half an hour later they're in a big sulk because somebody put the brand of peanut butter they don't like on the supper table. And this is how you get people who stop believing in God because of a deep personal trauma or tragedy – when someone they love is diagnosed with breast cancer or dies of meningitis. It's okay all the while it's other people's loved ones falling sick or dying: but if my religion is basically orientated around 'me', it ceases to mean anything once 'me' is too deeply threatened.

What Paul is saying in this passage from Romans is that something bigger than 'me' has to be included in the frame of reference. He is saying that we have a chance to live our lives in the light of something greater than ourselves – and that is the road to freedom.

When we live in the light of the Spirit, our lives are no longer guided by relative truth (the point of view of 'me') but by absolute truth (the way things are for us all; the pattern of creation; the Way, the Truth and the Life).

Once we live in the light of the Spirit, a tussle is set up between the self-interest of the 'me' and the bigger picture we see in the Spirit's light. This is where our free will comes in: it doesn't just happen to us, we have to choose it. Happiness, kindness, joy, peace, contentment, serenity – once we're off the ego trip and walking in the light, those things aren't just moods that come over us, they're choices we make, and we begin to understand they always were.

So the voice of our conscience belongs to every moment of free will; every opportunity to hearken to the Spirit that witnesses with our spirit to say, 'Actually, you know better that that' or 'Just forbear' or 'Be kind'. And in this passage from Romans, Paul asserts that the witness of the Spirit is also what allows us to step into our own royalty, to go through life with our heads held high – not in haughtiness but in dignity – because we are children of God. So the voice of our conscience is calling us to something noble and magnificent as well as understanding and forgiving and kind.

Paul also says here that this is a path of life:

> …He who raised Christ from the dead will also give life to
> your mortal bodies through his Spirit, who lives in you…
> For if you live according to the sinful nature, you will die;
> but if by the Spirit you put to death the misdeeds of the
> body, you will live, because those who are led by the Spirit
> of God are sons of God.

> *Romans 8:11, 13–14*

This belongs to the creation ordinance of things: 'In the beginning, God' (Genesis 1:1). Transformation and creation begin with Spirit and from there generate change on the material plane. So if we start with a free-will decision to open ourselves to God's Spirit, and stop living 'the gospel according to me', choosing instead to live in the light of something greater than ourselves, orientating ourselves with all the rest of nature around the Creator – then we shall step into life. If we try to live by tinkering with the externals (which is all the material plane is), pinning our faith on the flux of circumstances and the well-being of 'me', we have chosen death: because 'me' is only mortal; we rely on the Spirit to give us life. This is what Jesus meant when he said:

> For whoever wants to save his life will lose it, but whoever
> loses his life for me will find it. What good will it be for a
> man if he gains the whole world, yet forfeits his soul? Or
> what can a man give in exchange for his soul?

> *Matthew 16:25–26*

Some people argue that those who have not accepted Christ

as their saviour do not have free will; they are in bondage to the devil; since it is the Spirit who sets us free, only those who are filled with the Spirit have free will. That's a plausible thesis within a religious context, but it can't be true because it would preclude people from choosing Christ in the first place. Such a view is also at odds with the teaching in Romans 1:19–22:

> …What may be known about God is plain to them, because God has made it plain to them. For since the creation of the world God's invisible qualities – his eternal power and divine nature – have been clearly seen, being understood from what has been made, so that men are without excuse.
>
> For although they knew God, they neither glorified him as God nor gave thanks to him, but their thinking became futile and their foolish hearts were darkened. Although they claimed to be wise, they became fools…

Nature is orientated around the person of absolute truth – God: 'his eternal power and divine nature – have been clearly seen, being understood from what has been made' – which means that the predisposition for orientation towards God is already in our natural being, to which our conscience belongs, even before we activate the possibility of transformation in our lives by the renewal of our minds, through inviting the indwelling of the Spirit.

The voice of the conscience – the sat nav that calls us to the road of blessing – is something like a spring of water arising from the earth. It can become muffled and disguised by accretions of dirt and dead leaves: we have to keep it clear. This is another instance of the important role of habit in our lives. If we have the habit of listening to our conscience and following its requirements, we keep the sound of it clean and clear. If we are double-minded and pulled about by lesser concerns – not true to ourselves, not true to God, not loving to others and not respectful of the point of view of the rest of creation – then we create chaos in our mind and spirit; conflicting voices.

What begins in Spirit will show up in the material realm sooner or later: if our heads and hearts are chaotic and conflicted, our lives will visibly take on that character in time – not our individual lives only but our neighbourhoods and nations.

To get on the road of blessing, we have to allow the voice of our conscience to grow strong by paying attention to it; so that a purity and clarity develops within us and begins to manifest in our lives.

As we wait in confidence for our thoughts and intentions to materialize concretely in our lives, sometimes we wonder why the things we have focussed on don't always show up quickly in our lives – sometimes we have to wait and pray a long time. To understand that, we have to remember that in bringing about change through prayer we are operating in two different realms. We are starting from the spiritual realm which has no bounds or limitations and bringing our vision through into the more constricted material plane where the limitations of time and space apply. Therefore, though each spiritual impulse is really here as soon as our hearts and minds conceive it, there is a gestation period before it can be seen in the material world. God is eternal, and spiritual, and that means with God everything is Here and Now. Because we are in the material plane of the physical world, our senses need the buffer of time and space to stop us being swamped and overwhelmed. But time and space are not the way things actually are – they are the mode of our experience. Even in the material world, physicists know that our sub-atomic particles can move about the universe freely, both geographically and historically; they are not bounded by time and space.

The place where time and space touch eternity is the present moment. So our free-will choices for transformation rely on Moments. In all of us at any given time, the possibility for any of the other states is there in latent form. When we are choosing to step into the way of Spirit, the lower nature remains present, though dormant: if we are not watchful, we may slide back into that mode in another Moment of choice. But even when we are mired in the most deep and desperate sin, the state of grace is a latent possibility within us: all we have to do is choose, repent and ask – and in that Moment we step into absolute forgiveness and grace.

We can see one of those Moments in the story of the prodigal son. He sank as low as he could go. He contaminated his body, the temple of God's Spirit, with inappropriate sexual liaisons and intoxicants (note that word *toxic* in the middle of 'intoxicants'; it's basically a warning that people soaking up recreational drugs and booze are inadvertently poisoning themselves). He lived with pigs – representing the pits of uncleanness to the Jewish mind. The depths he had reached were signified by the description: 'He longed to fill his stomach with the pods that the pigs were eating, but no one gave him anything' (Luke 15:16). So even the *pigs* were superior to his condition in that moment.

Then, the story says: 'he came to himself' (verse 17, KJV). This is such a telling phrase. It shows that the moment of repentance, insight, enlightenment, is holistic in direction: what we are, is reconciled with what we ought to be; we are made more truly ourselves in choosing the Way, the Truth, the Life.

Allowing the voice of conscience to lead us into the road of blessing is a matter of both reinforcing our ability to hear and respond to that voice by setting in place daily the habit of obedience, and seizing as they arise the Moments when we 'come to ourselves'; the opportunities to step from one state of being into another; the simple choices that find our feet in the way of grace.

Direct leading accessed through prayer

I heard John Wimber say he knew only three prayers:
> 'Oh, God!'
> 'Help!'
> 'Oh, God – help!'

That's probably all we need. 'The name of the Lord is a strong tower; the righteous run to it and are safe' (Proverbs 18:10)

On the road of blessing, prayer is crucial for several things:

- Prayer links us up with energy/power immeasurably greater than our own.

- Prayer reorientates us towards God, and in so doing draws us into greater harmony with the rest of nature and humanity.

- Prayer unlocks permission, allowing us to take advantage of Moments of transformation.

- Prayer is the spiritual activity that will determine the nature of our material circumstances (not necessarily for comfort, but certainly for grace and love).

- Prayer allows our time/space environment to connect with God's eternal presence, and so in some senses allows us to transcend the limitations of time and space.

- Immersion in prayer is inherently transformative, not only promoting the peace and power of the Spirit of God within us, but improving the vibrational quality of our lives as they affect the lives of others.

This vibrational quality is important. All life is electro-magnetic, so every living thing has an electrical or vibrational field. Traditional pictures of saints show them with haloes round their heads, and that's an expression of the vibrational field emanating from them being golden and pure and holy.

Many instances from all around the world have been recorded of communities benefiting from reduced crime rates and more peaceful social interactions when people get together to meditate and pray. The vibrational field of holiness permeates the surrounding community, bringing peace and well-being.

I've often wondered to what extent the decline of monastic communities may have contributed to violence and unrest in society. In the neighbourhood where I lived most of my adult life, I saw several convents close as the nuns grew too old to administer them any longer. Because nuns live quietly, without drawing attention to themselves, their departure went mainly unnoticed by the neighbourhood around where they'd lived. But these had been powerhouses of prayer, and their loss will have made a profound difference.

Prayer taps us into the beating heart of God; it changes everything. When we pray, things connect up – people and books and articles and TV programmes come our way pointing us towards truth and light. When we pray, we find ourselves inexplicably in the right place at the right time. When we pray, even our inconsequential remarks are used as channels of grace – the word that someone else was longing to hear.

Prayer leads us into the road of blessing; and the road of blessing leads us deeper into prayer.

Chapter Three

❧

Understanding the Power of Blessing

You can put yourself in the way of blessing, to receive it; but you cannot earn it. God is gracious, and he loves to give. Though it is rich and heavy with consequences, life is emphatically not a system of rewards and punishments; for life streams forth from God, and God is love, and love by its nature can never be conditional. Approval is conditional. Love is unconditional. In the scriptures we read about many things that God approves of or abhors, but God's nature is love – we can take that for granted because it is granted; freely, permanently, unconditionally. God loves you, and every circumstance of your life is an expression of his love towards you, however bewildering and unlikely that may seem at the time. God loves you, and every moment of every day offers a way in to his love; and you can walk in his love, and so follow the way of blessing.

In the faith path of Hinduism, and to a more limited extent in Buddhism, and in New Age philosophy, there is teaching and discussion about karma. Each of these faith paths teaches some form (details vary) of reincarnation, and understands karma to play out over many lifetimes until the soul reaches the point of enlightenment where earthly lessons are no longer necessary and release from the wheel of birth and death is attained. Karma is the principle of cause and effect, reaping the harvest of what has been sown. Because of this, suffering in this life is sometimes seen as consequent upon misdeeds in a former life.

In some expressions of Hinduism, suffering can be ignored as the responsibility of the suffering individual – a consequence of former sin and an opportunity for present expiation and progress, to achieve future well-being and prosperity and ultimately bliss. Other expressions of Hinduism and Buddhism take a more compassionate and sophisticated view, incorporating the possibility that the suffering individual may be a teacher, saint, or bodhisattva, beyond the cycle of reincarnation but consenting to return for the purpose of teaching others compassion.

In Hinduism, Buddhism and New Age paths, compassion towards the suffering is also seen as good karma for oneself, contributing towards the refinement, enlightenment and edification of one's own soul. Asceticism is also seen as helpful in shaking the soul free of clinging attachments that would lead to sensuality and decadence, impeding the progress of the soul.

Judaism and Christianity also believe firmly in the harvest of consequences: *as you sow, so shall you reap*. The Old Testament of the Bible includes a system of thought espousing the understanding that obedience to the holy Law and command of God will bring prosperity, health, fertility and peace; whereas disobedience and apostasy will bring calamity, poverty, disease, barrenness and war. But it is important to understand that this is not the only strand of thought in the Old Testament.

At about the same time that Abraham, who was God's friend, came out of Ur in the Chaldees to make his way across the desert at God's beckoning, the prophet Zoroaster emerged in Persia. From his world-view grew one of the greatest world religions. Zoroastrianism became a powerful cultural influence throughout the Middle East, right through the time that Judaism was developing, persisting beyond the coming of Christ and the birth of the church until Muslim persecution decimated its numbers, reducing it to the marginal minority religion it is today. It is hard for us to imagine now, how profound an impact and influence Zoroastrianism had on the thought and culture of the ancient world.

Zoroaster believed that this world is torn by the battle for supremacy between two supernatural powers – the forces of light against the forces of darkness. Ahura Mazda was the name he gave to the deity of the light, and to the foe, the lord of darkness, he gave the name Angra Mainyu. In this system of thought, all aspects of life are drawn into the battle. Zoroaster taught that the earth at its inception was perfectly round and smooth – it was Angra Mainyu's mischief, and the battle for the earth, that had caused mountains and gorges to form. Zoroastrians believed that if Ahura Mazda won the battle, every valley would be exalted, every mountain and hill made low, and the rough places made smooth – made into a plain.

Ahura Mazda represented and commanded light, health, order, cleanliness, well-being, prosperity, open air and fire. Angra Mainyu was responsible for darkness, disease, dirt, disorder, calamity and burial under the earth.

Zoroaster taught that each of these deities controlled hierarchical ranks of supernatural beings – angels and archangels in the case of Ahura Mazda, and ranks of demons in the case of Angra Mainyu. Our beloved archangels' names – Gabriel, Raphael, Michael and Uriel – come from the Zoroastrian hosts of light. Humanity also found itself implicated in the battle, and the actions of everyone, no matter how lowly, influence the eventual outcome.

It takes little reflection to see what a powerful force for order, goodness, health and peace Zoroastrianism exerted in the world, with thousands of devotees channelling the detail of their everyday lives into the battle.

Known as a fire religion, Zoroastrian temples kept a perpetual flame burning as a sign of the power of Ahura Mazda. Birds, creatures of light and air, were revered; and Zoroastrians exposed their dead in high places to be picked clean by the birds of the air, rather than burying them in the bowels of the earth – the realm governed by Angra Mainyu.

Devoted to peace, well-being and order, Zoroastrianism was a benign and tolerant religion, and the emerging Hebrew people had cause for gratitude for its benevolence. Cyrus of Persia, the great Zoroastrian leader, had looked kindly upon the Jews; not only defending their right to return and rebuild the holy Temple at Jerusalem, but helping them generously with supplies and equipment to complete the task.

The book of Isaiah includes words of prophecy addressed towards Cyrus of Persia, expressing the understanding that because of his kindness towards Yahweh's chosen people, God looked with favour upon Cyrus, saw him as his anointed servant: 'I summon you by name and bestow on you a title of honour, though you do not acknowledge me.' (Isaiah 45:4)

But tactfully, delicately, diplomatically, Isaiah has a theological bone to pick with Cyrus, concerning the nature of God. Zoroastrian Cyrus believes that Deity is dual – opposing forces locked in combat, the outcome of which was by no means a foregone conclusion. This is not what Isaiah believed. It was not the faith of the patriarchs.

Noah trusted God, and listened to his call; and God saved and protected Noah and his family and the animals gathered into the ark, even as God simultaneously wiped the face of the earth clean of corrupt humanity. Abraham had walked with God as his friend, trusting him absolutely. He interceded with God over the fall of Sodom – and it was God who saved, but also God who destroyed. Israel (Jacob) struggled and fought with God; and it was God who disabled him, as well as God who blessed him and made him the person he was – gave him his name. Moses taught the people, 'The Lord our God, the Lord is One' (Deuteronomy 6:4): and as far as Isaiah was concerned, no rival existed to the all-supreme and all-encompassing nature of God. 'I am that I am', God had given as his name – unrivalled, self-determining, the destiny and first cause of all life.

Isaiah's prophecy to Cyrus of Persia, while respectful, humble, grateful, shines with confidence about the nature of God: 'I am the Lord, and there is no other' (Isaiah 45:5). He works with Cyrus' view of perfection – the smooth ball of the earth – with the glorious affirmation:

A voice of one calling:
'In the desert prepare the way for the Lord;
make straight in the wilderness
a highway for our God.
Every valley shall be raised up,
every mountain and hill made low;
the rough ground shall become level,
the rugged places a plain.
And the glory of the Lord will be revealed,
and all mankind together will see it.
For the mouth of the Lord has spoken.'

Isaiah 40:3–6

He asserts that this perfection is not the hard-won outcome of an uncertain battle, but the revelation of an inherent natural and supernatural order; the unique supremacy of God – echoed later for Christians in the miracles of Christ; the healing of sickness, the stilling of the storm ('Who can this be, that even the wind and the sea obey him?' – Matthew 8:27, NKJV).

Isaiah underlines for Cyrus that God is the God of the *wholeness* of life: his dominion is not over some aspects only, but over everything. All that happens to us arises from our relationship with the living God. There is nothing dualistic about our life and spirituality – it is holistic. The depths of the earth belong to God just as much as the heights of the heavens. Our trouble and sorrow are held in the hands of God as much as our well-being and prosperity:

> This is what the Lord says to his anointed,
> to Cyrus, whose right hand I take hold of
> to subdue nations before him
> and to strip kings of their armour,
> to open doors before him
> so that gates will not be shut:
> I will go before you
> and will level the mountains;
> I will break down gates of bronze
> and cut through bars of iron.
> I will give you the treasures of darkness,
> riches stored in secret places,
> so that you may know that I am the Lord,
> the God of Israel, who summons you by name.
> For the sake of Jacob my servant,
> of Israel my chosen,
> I summon you by name

and bestow on you a title of honour,
though you do not acknowledge me.
I am the Lord, and there is no other;
apart from me there is no God.
I will strengthen you,
though you have not acknowledged me,
so that from the rising of the sun
to the place of its setting
men may know there is none besides me.
I am the Lord, and there is no other.
I form the light and create darkness,
I bring prosperity and create disaster;
I, the Lord, do all these things.

Isaiah 45:1–7

There are no places where Isaiah's God cannot go; there is no boundary where his dominion stops, no experience through which he cannot accompany us:

Even to your old age and grey hairs
I am he, I am he who will sustain you.
I have made you and I will carry you;
I will sustain you and I will rescue you.

Isaiah 46:4

Again and again Isaiah insists on the unrivalled majesty of God:

This is what the Lord says –
Israel's King and Redeemer, the Lord Almighty:
I am the first and I am the last;
apart from me there is no God.

Isaiah 44:6

I am the Lord,
who has made all things,
who alone stretched out the heavens,
who spread out the earth by myself...

Isaiah 44:24b

To whom will you compare me or count me equal?
To whom will you liken me that we may be compared?

Isaiah 46:5

In understanding the power of blessing, it is important to bring into clear focus the biblical world-view; that there is no power but God's, no source but God, no destiny but God – he is the Lord, and there is no other.

The friendly relationship between the sons of Abraham and the sons of Zoroaster, and the perpetuation of powerful Zoroastrian influence well into the formative years of the early church, has imparted a cultural flavour to some Christian thought and some biblical texts, which has sunk out of our awareness now that Zoroastrians have so dwindled in number in the modern world.

We understand that as the apostle Paul resolutely held open the way in for the Gentiles, Hellenistic thought was added to the originally Jewish culture of the church's beginnings: but we usually fail to grasp that a significant proportion of the Gentile cultural aspect of the early church was not Greek but Zoroastrian, and that the long memory of the Jewish people remained friendly to Cyrus and his people.

The gospels are documents for the formation of disciples, written to allow the early Christians to understand who Jesus was, why he came, and how to appropriate and grow into his continuing presence in their midst. Each gospel is written not in a vacuum but into a pastoral context: and study of the gospel texts tells us something about the church into which each was written.

Matthew's gospel is often described as a very Jewish gospel, in which light is shed upon Jesus as fulfilling the Law of Israel, as holding firm in faithfulness where Israel had been unfaithful, as carrying through for the people of promise the hope of the Covenant.

But there was a Gentile presence in Matthew's congregation too, and their concerns become apparent in his gospel. Not only does Christ fulfil the seeking and aspiration of the Jews in Matthew's gospel – he is the fulfilment of the Gentile search as well. The magi of the birth narrative in Matthew are Zoroastrian, and they discern the Messiah by Zoroastrian means. Their Zoroastrian practice leads them to Christ, to whom they pay homage as their search is fulfilled in him; and this balances in the gospel with the fulfilling of the Law of Moses in the person of Jesus Christ.

So Zoroastrian thinking, with its dualistic tendencies, was alive and well as the Christian church took shape. Nothing is more powerful than the influences of which we remain unaware. Even today, there is a tendency towards dualism in Christian thought: a tendency to balance off Christ against Satan as opposing powers representing kingdoms locked in mortal combat, in which battle each of us plays a part. And though the church *teaches* that the victory is won, its people don't always *behave* as though they believe that – going in fear of demons or taint from other religions, weighed down by superstitious dread of the enemy's power.

I stand with Isaiah, with Abraham, with the Christ whose

victory on the cross is won. Life – with all its joys, terrors, delight, wonder, sorrow, frailty and complexity – belongs entirely to God.

In moving from the Old Testament to the New, we also encounter the Christ who comes to us – the advent of grace. 'My grace is sufficient for you,' Paul tells the Corinthians God said to him, 'for my power is made perfect in weakness' (2 Corinthians 12:9). We encounter the Gospel vision of salvation that not only *does not* have to be earned, it *cannot* be earned: we who were slaves to sin, in bondage to sin, are set free in Christ to new life and take hold of real and certain hope. Once this hope is in us, we can lay hold of it as a lifeline, and follow it along the way of blessing. It will become the factor that determines our experience of life, regardless of the external circumstances we pass through.

From the ancient religions of Hindusim and Zoroastrianism come the teachings of karma (the law of cause and effect) and the view of life as a battlefield in which all we do weighs in the scales towards the eventual outcome. Though these concepts have their place and resonate with our experience of what life is like, if we are a biblical people, then our understanding of blessing will be formed from the presuppositions that:

- Everything that happens to us comes from the hand of God and is part of our relationship with God – there are no boundaries to his reign of love.

- The law of cause and effect, of choice and consequence, of sowing and harvest, is dynamically transformed by the intervention of grace: God's undeserved favour poured into our lives through the saving death on the cross of Jesus Christ – which rent the temple veil, making access in the here and now into the heart of God. We do not have to travel there through many lifetimes: he has come to us himself.

When we grasp these two principles, we greatly enhance our capacity for optimism, trust and faith. Life becomes less rigid and fearful. We begin to experience God's kindness, and learn to see difficult times not as punishments or obstacles to faith, but as opportunities for growth and development into which God (whom we can always absolutely trust) is leading us by the hand – just as the Spirit took Jesus into the wilderness at the beginning of his ministry.

We can learn to look at the Book of Life in the same way as we are learning to look at the Bible. Instead of making ourselves into the supreme authority, evaluating, assessing, judging and categorizing everything that happens to us – pigeonholing everything as 'good' or bad', 'nice' or 'nasty', 'what I want' or 'what I don't want' – we can take the disciple's approach, asking, 'What can I learn from this?'; 'How might I apply the principles of blessing here?'; 'What does this circumstance need me to add, to make it better resemble Christ's Kingdom of Peace?'; 'Where are the springs of grace in this situation?'

If we assume from the beginning that life is good, because God's power is the only power and our lives are in his hands, we shall not waste time and energy in hand-wringing, resentment and indignation. Asking 'What is there here for me to learn and how can I help?' focuses the mind and brings calm, helping us to get the best out of any situation.

It's important to hold on to this even when we can see very clearly that our circumstances are of our own making. Shame and guilt are paralysing and time-consuming. So is anxiety.

If, for example, we have overspent on a foolish purchase and created financial difficulties for ourselves, it is natural to feel wretched and ashamed. But as quickly as possible, we should ask for the intervention of grace. God's great love has allowed us to get into this mess, the better to understand ourselves and learn what does and doesn't work. We have reaped the harvest of our stupid sowing. But God's love is unconditional, his forgiveness and grace are boundless. It doesn't matter if we messed up and got it wrong – the way things are is elastic enough to allow for our weakness and folly; we will be better and wiser and stronger for having made the mistake, if we learn from it and seek God's help to put it right. And, God's resources have not run out just because our judgment was off. We can ask him, and he will give us what we need to make things right again. Sometimes what we need is simply to get our act together and improve our grip on our finances – and God has the grace that is sufficient for us to do that too.

Not all the scary things that befall us are our own fault – we may be mistakenly arrested for a crime we didn't commit, or we may be diagnosed with a dreadful illness, or our teenage son may be killed in a traffic accident. Terrible things can happen at any time to anybody. When the worst befalls us, it helps immensely if we have already been practising the disciple's approach – asking ourselves, 'What can I do to love and serve in this place?', 'What are the lessons for me here?', 'Where are the springs of grace?'

To put this effectively into practice, so that even when we are pummelled by dreadful circumstances we can find the springs of grace on the road of blessing, here are the things we need to remember:

- What we put into the world will return to us.

- What we take refuge in, in turn will take refuge in us.

- Like calls to like.

- We get more of what we pay attention to.

- People who tell the truth can work miracles.

- Each of us is called to responsibility in his or her own life: no one else's.

What we put into this world will return to us

Cast your bread upon the waters, for after many days you will find it again.

Ecclesiastes 11:1

Do not judge, and you will not be judged. Do not condemn, and you will not be condemned. Forgive, and you will be forgiven. Give, and it will be given to you. A good measure, pressed down, shaken together and running over, will be poured into your lap. For with the measure you use, it will be measured to you.

Luke 6:37–38

With the measure you use, it will be measured to you— and even more. Whoever has will be given more; whoever does not have, even what he has will be taken from him.

Mark 4:24–25

Do not be deceived: God cannot be mocked. A man reaps what he sows.

Galatians 6:7

75

This is a firm biblical principle: it can be trusted. It can be puzzling when it doesn't seem to be coming true: when we see bad people (apparently) enjoying good things; when we see kind, gentle people taken advantage of or abused. But we should remember that the Bible is a holy book, and its insights come from the perspective of the Spirit.

One of the collects (short prayers) of the Church of England prays that we may 'so pass through things temporal that we finally lose not the things eternal'. The letter to the Hebrews (13:14) says, 'here we have no abiding city, but we look for the city that is to come'. This means that earth is not our original, permanent home. For now it is our home, and it is made by God and beautiful. It is important that we cherish and respect the earth God made, remembering that he has charged humankind with the responsibility of caring for the earth. But we are here for a brief sojourn only; we are destined for heaven. Heaven is not like earth. It is not determined by the boundaries of space and time – those are characteristic of the physical realm. Earth is physical, but heaven is spiritual. Jesus described it like this: 'When the dead rise, they will neither marry nor be given in marriage; they will be like the angels in heaven' (Mark 12:25).

Even the physical realm is not entirely constrained by time and space. Our subatomic particles can travel the universe, and travel in time.

Time and space are experiential conditions. We experience life as linear – one event succeeding another, as one bead comes after another in a necklace. We have to experience life like that, or our senses would be swamped and overwhelmed. If you could even open your senses to experience simultaneously everything that has happened in the room where you are sitting, it would be too much for you – it would crash your system. Your physical being requires that you experience life one event at a time.

But time is not really linear like that. Being, events – these are more like a bundle or a ball, and our subatomic particles can move about through them from place to place, time to time. God, who is and has eternal life, is beyond and behind and above time, as well as experienced by us in time. It is as though eternal life is everything in the present tense. That's why the only access we have to God is through the present moment. The present moment is the only place where history touches eternal life – because 'past' and 'future' have no meaning in eternal life; nor do 'there' or 'here' or 'away'. God is immanent as well as transcendent; he is with us – now. This moment now is the doorway to eternal life.

This means that the cause and effect of our choices are not always immediately present in time and space, even though in the eternal dimension they are already effective. Our experience of life is linear – we have to pass through the buffer of hours, days, weeks, to reach experientially the reality our choices have brought into being.

If you haven't thought about life in these terms before, it can seem a bit baffling – it needs some thinking over before it sinks in. A helpful metaphor is that of conception and birth. A child is conceived. Nine months go by before the child is born. But at three months'... six months'... eight months' gestation... the child is already there, just hidden from view. We talk about 'a new baby'; but the baby has already been with us for nine months before we meet him, before we see his face. The birth is the consequence of the fertilization; the baby is there from the moment of fertilization – but nine moons wax and wane before the baby is there for everyone to see.

So it is with our choices – our thoughts, attitudes, words and actions. Every word, thought, deed is a cause in the eternal dimension which will have an effect sooner or later in time; a seed already germinating, which will bear fruit one day. Everything we do is a choice for which we are responsible, and everything we choose has a consequence. The consequence is present the instant the choice is conceived; but because we are creatures of time and space, experiencing life as linear history, those consequences are not always immediately apparent. Sometimes there is a gestation period. But: 'Do not be deceived: God cannot be mocked. A man reaps what he sows' (Galatians 6:7). What you put into the world will return to you again.

What we take refuge in, in turn will take refuge in us

This is like a mirror image of the previous principle. Just as what we put out into the world will come back to us, so what we take into ourselves will out. It's the same underlying principle of sowing and harvesting; but this time the field in which we are sowing is our inner being, rather than the environment of our lives.

The Bible teaches us that we are temples of God's Holy Spirit, and it is our responsibility to keep the sanctuary of our inner being pure and holy. It would be a shocking thing to use a church, a holy temple, as a brothel, or to show pornographic movies, or as a gambling den or the scene of a drunken party. It would be a terrible thing to find a church exploiting the poor, or involved in corrupt business deals. Well, we are the church, and each one of us is a holy temple. It is our responsibility to keep our lives holy unto the Lord.

I remember going into a supermarket when the first series of Gillian McKeith's programme *You Are What You Eat* had been running for a few weeks. The fruit and vegetable section was almost stripped bare! The nation was waking up to the reality that the food they put in their mouths would directly affect not only their waistlines and physical condition, but also their energy levels, their mood and their libido. What we take into ourselves will make us well, or ill. We need sunshine, rest, fresh fruit and vegetables and whole grains. We need companionship, affirmation, love and encouragement. We need stimulus and a sense of purpose. We need a balance of work, rest and leisure.

What we put into ourselves will determine what we become. As far as the choice lies with us, we are wise to see to it that we eat, participate in, watch, read and listen to, only what is wholesome, pure and good.

In the subcontinent of India, there is a traditional system of medicine and nutrition known as Ayurveda. According to this tradition, food is divided into three types: sattvic, rajasic and tamasic. The word 'sattvic' comes from the same root as the Indian word for 'truth' – and in the word 'rajasic' we can see the word 'rajah' – a nobleman or patrician. So, sattvic food is light, fresh food that is pure and easily digested; it keeps us sweet and light and gentle. Rajasic food is more concentrated – hot and spicy and fried; it gives a more aggressive energy, suitable (within limits) to those whose work and responsibilities need a hard-headed, earthy, assertive approach. Tamasic food is bad news: stale, highly processed, intoxicating, heavy on the digestive system – it drains the body's energy, giving little back. 'Tamas' is the condition of darkness, dullness, inertia, sunk in materialism. The person who eats tamasic food ends up overloaded with toxins, tired and depressed.

In the Christian church, some of the teaching of the Bible has led us to strongly de-emphasize the importance of diet. The New Testament announces the Gospel of grace, bringing the Good News that it is by God's love and Christ's saving death that we are redeemed, not by adhering slavishly to dietary codes. Indeed, food will not save our souls! Even so, what we choose to eat is important, because our souls have nowhere to be expressed except through our physical being. Our bodies are temples of the Holy Spirit; how we treat them and what we bring into them should reflect our awareness of that. Not only do our dietary choices have political and environmental effects – some choices are compassionate, others horrifically cruel and destructive – but what we eat will affect our mood and temperament, making it harder or easier for us to be faithful in living out the Good News of Christ in the world.

A number of foods can affect our mental health, and we should take the trouble to educate ourselves about this. And there are some 'foods' – especially some beverages, whether alcoholic or soda – that contribute only two things to the world: fleeting pleasure and lasting trouble. They are a waste of God's money, that he has entrusted to our stewardship. Eve's mistake – 'it does look good to eat; and it does taste nice' – is characteristic of the whole human race!

What applies to food applies equally to the company we keep, the matters on which we allow our minds to dwell, the programmes we watch on television, the type of music we listen to and our reading material. These things settle into habits, and gradually our soul is formed. Part of our discipleship is to be informed and self-controlled in these areas; making the wise choices that will bless ourselves and others too.

What we take refuge in, will also take refuge in us.

Like calls to like

When my children went back into school after a couple of years of home education, I felt concerned lest they be bullied or badly influenced. Their grandfather, who had been a headmaster, made the observation that within a school, children will find their way to the others like themselves.

It is natural for like to cluster with like. In the skies, clouds form where other clouds are – you can make more clouds by creating clouds.

It's a matter of creating the conditions. Where water is, water will come. In dry, arid areas, planting trees will eventually encourage rain and hold onto the water in the landscape; once the conditions are set, the rainfall can happen.

An elderly friend of mine had made changes in his garden as his energy for digging and pruning waned. He had the trees cut down, and the bushes grubbed out. He erected a fence instead of the hedge that had bordered his garden before. The house door opened onto an area paved with concrete slabs, which gave onto a lawn kept mown short. A concrete path divided the lawn, edged with neatly weeded flower beds in which tulips, daffodils and Sweet Williams grew. Very orderly. One day as I sat chatting with him over a cup of tea, he remarked sadly, 'It's odd. We don't have birds visiting our garden like we used to, even though we put bread out on the bird table there.'

You have to set the conditions, and he'd just taken all his away. Plant trees, grow shrubs that the insects love to visit, allow some leaf cover and a little wildness; then the birds will

81

come. At first just a few, but word gets around among birds, like calls to like, and soon the garden will be full of birdsong on a spring morning.

It is the same in our spiritual walk. The people we become will draw to us others of like mind. If we choose well and live faithfully, we will be strengthened and encouraged by those who draw alongside us – and in turn we can strengthen and encourage them.

We set the conditions for this to happen by doing what Jesus said of himself: 'I tell you the truth, the Son can do nothing by himself; he can do only what he sees his Father doing, because whatever the Father does the Son also does' (John 5:19).

Our daily walk of prayer and discipleship, fed by a familiarity with scripture, should look deeply into the circumstances of daily life to discern where and how the Father is at work through his Holy Spirit. Once we see what he is doing, how his grace is flowing, we join in with that – setting the conditions in our lives for Kingdom people to gather and the work of the Kingdom to increase.

The beautiful monastic community at Taizé, drawing thousands and thousands of young people from all over the world to make pilgrimage and touch the living sense of God's presence, began with a germ of vision: for a community where 'kindness of heart would be a matter of practical experience, and where love would be at the heart of all things'. Years of praying in solitude and small numbers, into that vision of love, set the conditions for the wonderful gatherings and international fellowship that later flowered in that place. Frère Roger prayed and listened, understood what God was saying and calling him to do, and went with that in faithfulness. After that, what was needed was not extra effort but faithfulness and perseverance; the outcome then happened naturally, because Frère Roger had put himself in the flow of God's will – he was on the road of blessing.

After the wonderful passage about putting on the whole armour of God, in the letter to the Ephesians, come these words of wisdom: 'And pray in the Spirit on all occasions with all kinds of prayers and requests. With this in mind, be alert and always keep on praying for all the saints' (Ephesians 6:18). Three things are in this short text: pray in the Spirit, be alert, and keep going.

Our prayers and requests are to be made *in the Spirit*: that is to say, they are not to be our own bright ideas, but according to the leading of God's voice calling us to pray. I was in church one Sunday when a flu epidemic had been causing alarm everywhere. Our preacher exhorted us to be the kind of calm, believing people who would offer a good witness in our society. When it came to the intercessions, the intercessor for the day led us along such lines as: 'We pray for everyone affected by the flu, and ask that maybe somehow our response might be that little bit different.' Good try, and full marks for paying attention to the preacher – but that is *not* an example of praying in the Spirit. Our prayer should be focused, specific, believing and convinced.

Prayer is often muddled with kind wishes, and offered in ignorance of how powerful it can be. Prayer for good weather at the summer fête is offered, but without beforehand seeking the Lord about the weather: because weather can indeed be altered by prayer and by commanding in the Name of Jesus, just as he stilled the storm. And there's a responsibility that goes with this. If there have been three weeks of drought and the farmers are crying out to God for rain, are we quite sure we are flowing with the will of God in asking for fine weather for the fête? If in doubt, don't pray for something you think will be vaguely nice, pray to know the mind of God and then pray in the Name of Jesus with full confidence.

Or someone may ask the Lord 'that Elsie will continue to improve in health and make a full recovery, if it be thy will'. Well, is it his will? If it is, go to the prayer with confidence and cut out the 'if it be thy will'. If you don't know, ask and pray until you do, and then pray with confidence. This is really important, because our prayer makes a difference.

When my previous husband, Bernard, was dying, I asked everybody to pray. But I requested that they please *not* pray for him to be healed, because his soul was turned towards death and the Lord was calling him home – it was his time. I asked that they pray for God's peace and upholding, and for a speedy and gentle release. So they did that, and we got what we asked for. It was the sweetest, most uplifting journey of grace imaginable. On his way out of this world, he was upheld and supported on every side, and in his passing he found Christ for himself and for real. But if the faithful had been praying in all different directions at once, we should not have had the sustained push in the direction of the flow of what the Father was doing.

Power in prayer is about aligning ourselves with the direction of the Father's will, and putting our effort there.

Like calls to like, as soon as conditions are set. 'They asked him "where, Lord?" and he said to them, "Where the body is, there will the eagles gather"' (Luke 17:37).

Jesus said: 'I tell you the truth, if you have faith and do not doubt... you can say to this mountain, "Go, throw yourself into the sea," and it will be done. If you believe, you will receive whatever you ask for in prayer' (Matthew 21:21–22).

As well as making our prayers *in the Spirit*, Ephesians 6:18 tells us to *be alert*. Jesus told us to 'watch and pray' (Mark 13:33, 14:38; Luke 21:36). This is about holding ourselves in readiness, keeping a short account with God, so that we haven't got baggage to deal with, relationships to sort out and old issues to set right. It's also about paying attention to what is going on, staying honest and pure in our hearts so that we read the signs of the times with a mind uncorrupted by the reign of Mammon that spreads so extensively through our society. It's about noticing how people are feeling, how things are with their souls. When we intercede for someone, we can ask them what they would like God to do for them (because that's what Jesus used to ask people); and we should also ask God to place into our hearts and minds what the need is, so that our intercession is right on the nail. And God will do this, we are promised it. 'If any of you lacks wisdom, he should ask God, who gives generously to all without finding fault, and it will be given to him' (James 1:5).

So we *pray in the Spirit*, we *keep alert*, and we *always keep on praying for all the saints*. Luke's gospel says Jesus taught his disciples that 'they should always pray and never give up' (Luke 18:1). That's why it's important to have sought the Father's will first of all. Think how much time you might waste if you set yourself to 'always pray and never give up', but God was doing something completely different and you were barking up the wrong tree entirely.

When you set the conditions, in life and in prayer, and hold steady to your course, in time like will call to like, and blessing will come to you.

We get more of what we pay attention to

One of our oldest prayers of blessing, Aaron's blessing, asks God to lift up the light of his countenance upon us: 'The Lord bless you and keep you; the Lord make his face shine upon you and be gracious to you; the Lord turn his face towards you and give you peace' (Numbers 6:24–26 NIV). Make his face shine upon us... turn his face towards us: in other words – *look* at us! Where the Lord turns his face, what he looks at, will be blessed:

> And I will turn my face towards you and make you fruitful, and multiply you, and establish my covenant with you.
>
> *Leviticus 26:9 Darby Translation*

> ... your sins have hidden his face from you...
>
> *Isaiah 59:1*

> My heart says of you, 'Seek his face!' Your face, Lord, I will seek.
>
> *Psalm 27:8*

> ... we know that when he appears, we shall be like him, for we shall see him as he is.
>
> *1 John 3:2b*

> ... when perfection comes, the imperfect disappears...
> Now we see but a poor reflection as in a mirror; then we shall see face to face.
>
> *1 Corinthians 13:10, 12*

So we see that blessing is about God's face being turned towards us, his gaze resting upon us. Blessing a situation or person involves focusing upon them.

In the Bible, blessing always implies increase, fertility, prosperity – life and new life. Where there is no blessing, things become arid and barren; crops wither away, promise fails to fulfil its potential, emptiness, death and atrophy are characteristic. We keep in mind that this does *not* mean God is not with the poor and does not love them; it does *not* mean that infertility is a sign that God has withdrawn his blessing from a couple; it does *not* mean that in times of hardship and loss God is absent. When we read the Bible, it is important to read each text within the context of the whole. As we have already considered, the Bible teaches that the whole of life – both times of happiness and ease, and times of sorrow and hardship – is God's good gift to us, bringing the means by which our discipleship in the faith is to be developed.

This is in fact how we turn around our circumstances and direct them onto the road of blessing. If our material means are scarce, it is an opportunity for our faith to grow, as we turn to God in trust and experience his miraculous provision. If our community experiences sickness and death, it is an opportunity for our compassion and kindness to grow, and the bonds of love between us to be strengthened. If people in our community fall upon hard times, it is a chance for the others to be generous to them, sheltering the shorn lamb from the wind. So our job as disciples is to see that we remain on the road of blessing – making sure that poverty in one area is balanced by riches in another, lack in one area rescued by plenty in another.

So the potential and opportunity for blessing are all

around us in every circumstance of our lives – the darker the night, the brighter the light appears – but the characteristic of blessing is increase; growth, multiplication.

If we join together these two biblical principles – that blessing results from focus, and is characterized by increase – then we arrive at what is also a matter of ordinary observation: what you focus on will increase. What you pay attention to, you get more of.

I expect you already know the old Cherokee story about a grandfather describing human nature to his grandson as the struggle for supremacy between two wolves. One is a bad wolf, full of anger and hate, the other a gentle, good wolf. When the grandson asks which wolf will win, the old man replies, 'The one I feed.' This is another manifestation of the same principle of blessing: what you pay attention to, you get more of. A wise friend of mine said to me: 'Expectations are like stray cats – if you don't want 'em, don't feed 'em.'

What you feed, what you dwell upon, what you look at and think about – where you put your attention – will grow and strengthen in your life. You are made in God's image, and the light of your countenance will bless what it falls upon.

A conundrum arises here. How can we bless what God is not blessing? We are made in the image of God, with the power to bless; but what if we are choosing to put our attention, the gaze of our soul, on corrupt and unworthy objects of focus – feuds and grudges, jealousies and resentments, for example?

If we put the principles together, we can see what happens. Imagine I have had a disagreement with a friend. Tempers have become frayed and hard words have been said. I feel wounded and upset. That's okay; it's part of being human – relationships are dynamic and people are emotional beings. The important thing is what I do about it next. Maybe I bring it to the Lord and ask his forgiveness for my part in the disharmony, go to my friend and apologize; my friend also apologizes, we forgive one another; and the relationship is not only mended, it is strengthened.

Alternatively, maybe I sulk and brood, reliving again and again the conversation, getting more and more indignant and resentful, recalling to mind other things of similar nature I've seen my friend do and say. I imagine confronting her, and mentally rehearse exactly what I'd like to say to her. I take refuge in resentment – and resentment takes refuge in me, putting down the root that will develop into a bitter grudge. I sprinkle my day with anger and bitter thoughts, and am snarky and rude to everyone I meet. What I sow, I reap; they take offence and are snarky and rude right back to me. While I do the ironing I thump away with the hot iron, muttering to myself about how unreasonable my friend is. I am not concentrating on the task in hand, and I burn myself, which puts me in even more of a rage. So I am getting more of what I am putting my attention on: the offence. Where I am resting the light of my countenance, I am seeing growth. The more I feed that wolf, the fatter it gets. The more I dwell on it, the deeper it works into my soul.

But God does not bless resentment and grudges. God will not rest his eyes upon mean-spiritedness and bad temper. 'And we know that all things work together for good to them that love God' (Romans 8:28, KJV). So basically, I am wasting my time in directing my energy into attitudes God cannot bless. I am creating blocks to 'all things working together for good' by giving my energy to a focus other than the order of God's loving purposes. The prophet Hosea describes it like this:

> They set up kings without my consent; they choose
> princes without my approval.
> With their silver and gold they make idols for themselves
> to their own destruction...
> They sow the wind and reap the whirlwind.
> The stalk has no head; it will produce no flour.
> Were it to yield grain, foreigners would swallow it up.
> Israel is swallowed up;
> now she is among the nations like a worthless thing.
>
> *Hosea 8:4, 7–8*

To use my energy to bless what God does not bless, to look where God is not looking, to send the flow of my soul's energy along a direction different from the flow of God's Spirit, is to make an idol. Because my attention should be on him. My conduct and behaviour, my choices and attitudes, should all proceed from focusing on God. God is what I'm supposed to be focusing on. My gaze, my blessing, my focus, should be directed towards him. Then, as I look at him and he looks at me, we set up a loop of blessing which is sovereign over every circumstance of life.

If I take my attention off him to focus on what is mean or greedy or unkind, then it's as if my soul springs a leak; the blessing loop is broken and the energy drains away. Resentment, anxiety, anger, jealousy, avarice – these are all very draining and debilitating, as well as destructive. They sow the wind, and they reap the whirlwind: a crop of emptiness and a harvest of destruction.

When I say that my attention should be on God, I mean that my life should orientate around him. When I'm cooking the dinner or choosing the groceries or bathing the baby or altering a skirt, my mind is on that job. I don't go through life in a goofy 'Jesus is my boyfriend' dream, gazing on the fair loveliness of the Lord while the toast burns and the porridge boils over. I ask myself, 'What have I been sent here to do?'; checking with the Master what my role and mission is to be as my circumstances evolve and change. And I know that there are certain principles that I can always apply with confidence: 'He has showed you, O man, what is good. And what does the Lord require of you? To act justly and to love mercy and to walk humbly with your God' (Micah 6:8). The Bible is full of guidance, too many instances to quote, about how to live a good and holy life. If I familiarize myself with the scriptures, I know how to orientate my life around God, know what it means in daily practice to fix my gaze steadfastly upon him. 'The fruit of the Spirit is love, joy, peace, patience, kindness, goodness, gentleness, faithfulness, self-control' (Galatians 5:22–23).

So the *effective* way to use our blessing energy is to watch what the Father is doing and take our cue from him. That is the road of blessing. What we put our attention into we will get more of. If we put our attention into grabbing and getting and greed, then yes, our material circumstances will be enhanced; but that isn't blessing. It's necessary to be discerning about this, because there is an important distinction to be made. It is true that the Bible expresses blessing in terms of increase and prosperity, but consider this too:

> Woe to those who plan iniquity, to those who plot evil on their beds!
> At morning's light they carry it out because it is in their power to do it. They covet fields and seize them, and houses, and take them.

They defraud a man of his home, a fellow-man of his inheritance.

Micah 2:1–2

Woe to you who add house to house and join field to field till no space is left and you live alone in the land.

Isaiah 5:8

The prosperity and increase that the Bible describes as blessing is a state of holistic balance that incorporates all of human society and the whole of creation. Walking the road of blessing is about learning 'in all circumstances to be content' (Philippians 4:11, my paraphrase). You are blessed when you know you have enough:

I know what it is to be in need, and I know what it is to have plenty. I have learned the secret of being content in any and every situation, whether well fed or hungry, whether living in plenty or in want. I can do everything through him who gives me strength.

Philippians 4:12–13

The life of blessing is about being generous because our gaze is filled with the generosity of God; being at peace because we know ourselves loved by God; being content because we rest upon the provision of God's kindness.

Ambitious empire-building is not part of God's plan for us. Status symbols and expensive luxury and looking with a speculative eye on the common land and the forests are not within God's will for us. Trawling the sea with vast nets for every little fish that swims there is not resting in God's provision. Cutting down virgin rainforest to make garden furniture and cramming growth-accelerated birds into broiler houses for a fat profit has no part in the scriptural vision of what blessing means.

The affluence of Mammon is a sick parody of the abundance of God's love; there are some Christians too self-deceived to tell the difference. As we follow the road of blessing, choosing where to put our attention, what to grow by applying our focus there, we have to guard against greed and ambition and stay lowly; resting in contentment, humility, and looking for the way of littleness where Christ can always be found.

People who tell the truth can work miracles

Here is something amazing that Jesus said to his disciples (and we are his disciples too, so it also holds good for us). Read it carefully, and stay with his words for a moment. Ask yourself: do I believe this?

> Don't you believe that I am in the Father, and that the Father is in me? The words I say to you are not just my own. Rather, it is the Father, living in me, who is doing his work. Believe me when I say that I am in the Father and the Father is in me; or at least believe on the evidence of the miracles themselves. I tell you the truth, anyone who has faith in me will do what I have been doing. He will do even greater things than these, because I am going to the Father. And I will do whatever you ask in my name, so that the Son may bring glory to the Father. You may ask me for anything in my name, and I will do it.
>
> *John 14:10–14*

Now think about this conversation in Mark's gospel, that happened after the Transfiguration, when Jesus came down from the mountain and healed the boy who suffered convulsions:

> '… But if you can do anything, take pity on us and help us.'
>
> '"If you can"?' said Jesus. 'Everything is possible for him who believes.'
>
> Immediately the boy's father exclaimed, 'I do believe; help me overcome my unbelief!'
>
> *Mark 9:22b–24*

And add to those two texts these words:

> And we know that in all things God works for the good of those who love him, who have been called according to his purpose. For those God foreknew he also predestined to be conformed to the likeness of his Son, that he might be the firstborn among many brothers. And those he predestined, he also called; those he called, he also justified; those he justified, he also glorified.
>
> What, then, shall we say in response to this? If God is for us, who can be against us?
>
> *Romans 8:28–31*

Very often when we read the scriptures, it's just 'the Bible': holy, to be revered, yes. Something we say is true from cover to cover. The authority that orders our lives, we say. So – where are the miracles?

I think if we simply took those three texts that I have quoted here, and went to stay in a quiet place – a mountain cabin, or a retreat centre that offered solitude and silence – and lived with those texts for a month, they would turn our lives upside down.

I have been going to church all my life, and listened to no end of sermons, and lost count of the Bible studies and home groups I have attended. In all of them, I have heard, when you take it down to basics, two teachings about Jesus. Firstly, I have been taught that he was the same as us in his weakness and vulnerability – in his tears, his hunger and thirst, his weariness, his grief and his pain. Secondly, that in respect of his power and authority, his purity and holiness, integrity, humility and wisdom – he is *different* from us. Most of the sermons I have listened to have employed the strategy of instancing our thoughts, responses, feelings and actions, then saying that they are all wrong and that Jesus would do/say/feel/act in a different way. I think this approach is intended to be humble and lowly; avoiding pridefulness and arrogance, conceit. But I think also, it is not what the scriptures say.

These scriptures are saying that Jesus is *the same* as us (in every way except sin – Hebrews 4:15), the firstborn among many brothers. These texts say that, if we have faith in Jesus, everything is possible for us! That we can expect miracles just as he did, and even greater miracles than those! Is this still the same Bible by whose authority your life is governed? So, where are the miracles?

I have puzzled often over this question, asking myself, *why* did the winds and the waves obey Christ's words? *Why* did the demons and the illnesses disperse at his command? *Why* did his dying effect reconciliation, opening in the cross a crossing place, a way through from life to death and back again, through the veil that separated earth from heaven? I have come to the conclusion that the answer lies in his words: 'I am the way and the truth and the life. No one comes to the Father except through me' (John 14:6).

Jesus said this really important thing about the Holy Spirit: 'when he, the Spirit of truth, comes, he will guide you into all truth. He will not speak on his own; he will speak only what he hears' (John 16:13).

This witnesses to how the road of blessing works; by aligning our lives with the flow of the Father's will, choosing and doing what is in harmony with the way he is moving. The Holy Spirit will not act as a loose cannon, making things up randomly and leading us unpredictably: the Holy Spirit will lead us in the flow of what God is doing, where God is moving – and thus what we choose, do and say will become effective, transformative, and holy. And the Spirit will do this through the medium of Truth. He will show us truth, take us by the hand to lead us into truth: truth is what will become for us the way of blessing.

I think we can understand from these texts that unless truth, at every level and in every sense, is what conditions our lives, we shall not progress significantly along the road of blessing.

In the Bible, the concept of 'the word' is of central importance. God is described as creating the universe by his Word: 'God said, "Let there be light," and there was light' (Genesis 1:3). Jesus, who is the Way, the Truth and the Life, is described in John's gospel as being the eternal Word of God incarnate (John 1:1, 14, 18). The Word of God – such a big concept, holding within it everything from the creative, healing and redeeming power of God the Father, to the person of Jesus himself. And when Jesus speaks, his word heals, exorcises, exerts authority over the wild forces of nature. Why? Because his word is truth, and truth is reality, and everything that is real flows with reality.

In his miracles, Jesus didn't overturn or work against the laws of physics: rather, he was interacting with the universe at the *causative* level; which is what made his word inevitably effective. For the causative level of the universe is the Word of God – and the Word of God is always true; it is always truth.

We also can find ourselves hitting the vibration of the making of things if we become aligned with truth, with God's holy word – absolute reality and authenticity, expressed uniquely in his Son Jesus, who opens for us the living way into all truth.

When God calls himself 'I am that I am', it is about a state of being in which reality, authenticity and truth are at the neat, raw, absolute level; undiluted by compromise, prevarication or pretending. Jesus is not interested in his image, for 'He is the image of the invisible God' (Colossians 1:15). And the letter to the Colossians continues:

> He is the image of the invisible God, the firstborn over
> all creation. For by him all things were created: things in
> heaven and on earth, visible and invisible, whether thrones
> or powers or rulers or authorities; all things were created
> by him and for him. He is before all things, and in him
> all things hold together. And he is the head of the body,
> the church; he is the beginning and the firstborn from
> among the dead, so that in everything he might have the
> supremacy. For God was pleased to have all his fullness
> dwell in him, and through him to reconcile to himself all
> things, whether things on earth or things in heaven, by

making peace through his blood, shed on the cross.

Once you were alienated from God and were enemies in your minds because of your evil behaviour. But now he has reconciled you by Christ's physical body through death to present you holy in his sight, without blemish and free from accusation – if you continue in your faith, established and firm, not moved from the hope held out in the gospel. This is the gospel that you heard and that has been proclaimed to every creature under heaven...

Colossians 1:15–23

'Every creature', we notice in passing – not humankind alone.

So through the reconciliation brought about by his death on the cross, Christ has become central to an indissoluble unity, all things held together in one redeemed whole, through which life flows from his presence at the centre. And Christ is the Word of God, and the Word of God is what speaks things into life, and the nature of the Word of God is truth.

We find further guidance about the central importance of truth in the letter of James:

If any of you lacks wisdom, he should ask God, who gives generously to all without finding fault, and it will be given to him. But when he asks, he must believe and not doubt, because he who doubts is like a wave of the sea, blown and tossed by the wind. That man should not think he will receive anything from the Lord; he is a double-minded man, unstable in all he does.

James 1:5–8

Double-mindedness is the antithesis of truth. Jesus says that the devil is 'a liar and the father of lies' (John 8:44), and teaches that those who lie are the children of the devil. The devil can destroy, but cannot create. God's Word, the outbreath of his I-am-that-I-am being of pure self-defining, self-actualizing authenticity and truth, has nothing of a lie within it: God is who he is – the origin and definition of truth.

This is why Jesus had such a visceral reaction against hypocrisy: because hypocrisy is travelling at full speed ahead away from the word of blessing, away from honesty and authenticity and reality; away from truth and therefore out of the flow of the Holy Spirit and out of the road of blessing.

If we are living in double-mindedness, hypocrisy and lies, we fall out of the place of God's creative Word, so our words become empty, and nature sees no reason to obey them. The reason we cannot calm the wind and waves, heal the sick and raise the dead is not because Jesus was a one-off freak whom nobody could possibly begin to emulate, but because we are not making the choice that he did to stand in the place of absolute truth, single-minded, single-hearted, one hundred per cent honest, with no vestige of a lie in his being anywhere. Anyone who lives like that will hit the resonance of God's creation, and the living forces of nature will shape up around their words, for their words will be words of making, like Christ's words were.

The bad news is that the church is as far from this as another galaxy. Consider this text from 1 John 4 (verses 16–20):

> And so we know and rely on the love God has for us. God
> is love. Whoever lives in love lives in God, and God in
> him. In this way, love is made complete among us so that
> we will have confidence on the day of judgment, because

in this world we are like him. There is no fear in love. But perfect love drives out fear, because fear has to do with punishment. The one who fears is not made perfect in love. We love because he first loved us. If anyone says, 'I love God,' yet hates his brother, he is a liar. For anyone who does not love his brother, whom he has seen, cannot love God, whom he has not seen.

These verses bring into light the secret by which miracles happen. The nature of God is love; so to flow with his creative Spirit means that we also must be loving – full of love, overflowing with love, our first and every instinct being loving. Love is kind and protective and forgiving and gentle and sensitive. When we are loving like that, our fear is dispersed. People are not afraid of what they love. This is partly because love is the greatest thing there is, and the greater is never afraid of the lesser. When we love completely, we are no longer afraid even though we are more vulnerable to hurt. We become like Jesus. When we are no longer afraid, we do not need to lie any more, or pretend. Lies belong to anxiety and a sense of inadequacy. Lies proliferate where people are afraid of being found out, when they are ashamed, when they have reason to believe they will be attacked. So where love is, truth will increase.

The church in general is not an environment that encourages truth, because it has been too focused on rules and because its approach has fostered a tendency to guilt. Anxious to fit in, and afraid of being shunned or excluded, many – most, even – church members pretend or are silent about matters of life and belief, so that they can continue to be included in the group. This is natural human behaviour, but it is incompatible with love, because it is innately fearful, and it is incompatible with miracles, which rely on truth.

The reason miracles need truth is associated with the first creation verse in Genesis: 'God said, "Let there be light," and there was light' (1:3). The Word of God is powerful and effective. In the letter of James (5:16), we come across that idea again: 'Therefore confess your sins to each other and pray for each other so that you may be healed. The prayer of a righteous man is powerful and effective.'

Because we are made in the image of God, and in our creation ordinance we have been given dominion over nature, our Word has the same creative power. The reason I say 'Word' with a capital 'W' is because I mean something more than just speech. God's Word is more than just his speech, because there is no hypocrisy in God. We have such a strong tendency to double-mindedness, we are so fragmented by sin, that it is difficult for us to conceptualize this. God describes himself, names himself as 'I am that I am': he is all of a piece with no cross-currents or contradictions. The heart of the Jewish Law is the *Shema* (Deuteronomy 6:4): 'Hear, O Israel: The Lord our God, the Lord is one.'

Jesus prayed for the household of faith: 'Holy Father, protect them by the power of your name – the name you gave me – so that they may be one as we are one' (John 17:11b). Complete unity of being and purpose is the objective here (it's worth looking up John 17 and really getting into the whole prayer to absorb what Jesus is asking). As the Father is in Jesus and Jesus is in the Father, so we are to be in Jesus and his Spirit is to be in us; therefore we, by the adoption of grace and the power of his indwelling Spirit, are to be completely in the Father. No separation, no division. We can be kept safe by the power of God's name – *I am that I am* – which expresses the absolute truth and authenticity of his being. This is in the book of Proverbs too: 'The name of the Lord is a strong tower; the righteous hasten to take refuge within it, and they are safe there' (18:10, my paraphrase).

Now this being safe in God's name is not a matter of creeds and doctrines. It's not about tribal religious beliefs, picking the big strong God, not the little weak gods, and lining up behind our one and obeying the rules of his club. It's nothing to do with whether people who have been married before can be married in church or whether women can become bishops or whether there are animals in heaven or whether our priests are in the apostolic succession or whether it's permissable to go to the supermarket for milk on a Sunday. Discussion of all those things is interesting and has its place, but the safe place of God's name is something else entirely.

God's being is love, and from love proceeds truth which is without fear. God's holy name, *I am that I am*, expresses the unprevaricating and indivisible unity of his being in which there are neither fear nor lies.

Therefore, when God speaks, his Word is at one with everything about him – no contradictions, no pretending. So all that proceeds from him is one thing – his truthful love. So Jesus, who proceeds from him, is all love and is the same as his words of creation – 'the Lord our God, the Lord is one'. Because of this, the creation can trust and obey him, and lines up immediately according to his Word.

When we speak, if we are double-minded, the universe, the creation, doesn't always know what to do – our Word is not always in accord with our words. We pray for what we have no intention of putting into practice in our lives; unity in the church perhaps, or social justice, or world peace. But our prayers can't come true, because the universe looks to see what our mind, our intention, our Word (what proceeds from our being, what *I am that I am* we are) is, and finds only mixed messages. We pray for peace while holding a grudge against our parents. We pray for social justice while buying goods produced in sweatshops. We pray for unity in the church, then leave our congregation because we can't have our own way. How could our prayers be answered? Our prayers are all over the place. Our words pray one thing, our lives proclaim another – how can the universe line up in obedience to our will? As Paul pointed out in 1 Corinthians 13:1, I can pray in any human language there is, and even in the language of angels – but if I am without love my words are no more than a 'sounding brass, or a tinkling cymbal' (KJV).

When we enter God's name, his *I am that I am*, we take refuge in his love. What we take refuge in will also take refuge in us – so his love begins to grow inside us. Where love is, truth will flourish. Where truth is, double-mindedness is no longer. And once we are single-minded – living, speaking, being, believing all of a unity – we shall see miracles. Because our Word (our actions, speech, thoughts and life) – the Word of we who have dominion over nature and are made in the image of God – will be powerful and effective; we shall send out no more mixed messages, and nature will know what to do.

Sometimes when I am writing, I read through what I have written to my family. They are people of faith and wisdom, and their comments always help. My daughter Grace was sitting with me feeding her three-month-old baby Michael as I finished these paragraphs about the connection between truth and miracles, and I read them back to her. She listened carefully, and then she said: 'But what should people do if this is too hard for them?' What a good question!

The road of blessing is of its nature dynamic, not static – it's a road, not a place, a direction, not a destination. We are all learners as well as teachers on this Earth – that's why we're here. Not even the best of us gets everything right every time. As a friend once said to me: 'I do my best; and when I get it wrong, God forgives me.' We fall short. The important thing about the faith journey is not so much where it's at right now but where it's headed. What direction are you travelling in? If, even though there be many bends in the road and it's a winding way, you are travelling generally into love and truth and good faith, then you are on the road of blessing; miracles will attend you.

Each of us is called to responsibility in his or her own life: no one else's

'In those days people will no longer say, "The fathers have eaten sour grapes, and the children's teeth are set on edge." Instead, everyone will die for his own sin; whoever eats sour grapes – his own teeth will be set on edge.

'The time is coming,' declares the Lord, 'when I will make a new covenant with the house of Israel and with the house of Judah. It will not be like the covenant I made with their forefathers when I took them by the hand to lead them out of Egypt, because they broke my covenant, though I was a husband to them,' declares the Lord.

'This is the covenant that I will make with the house of Israel after that time,' declares the Lord. 'I will put my law in their minds and write it on their hearts. I will be their God, and they will be my people. No longer will a man

teach his neighbour, or a man his brother, saying, "Know
the Lord," because they will all know me, from the least of
them to the greatest,' declares the Lord. 'For I will forgive
their wickedness and will remember their sins no more.'

Jeremiah 31:29–34

The Jewish religion in which Jesus grew up placed a very strong
emphasis on community. The Jewish people were the People
of God as a nation: to be born as one of their number was to
be born as one of God's own people. The teachings of the Old
Testament in the Law and the Prophets encourage loyalty to
God and loyalty to each other. The Jews were not to neglect
or forget their poor and struggling members, but give them
a chance, help them along, and look upon them with mercy.
There was a clear boundary between Jew and Gentile; this
protective and charitable attitude was not required towards
Gentiles – the people of God in the Old Testament were
fierce and warlike, and victory in battle was part of the deal in
belonging to God.

In the thinking of the Old Testament there is a blurring
of the individual and the community. 'Israel' is a man (Jacob)
but also a tribe. When an individual is described as somebody's
son, as for example Jephthah is described as a son of Gideon,
it is not quite clear if he is in our modern sense the son of
the man Gideon, or if what is meant is that he belongs more
loosely to the tribe of Gideon. Isaac is described as Abraham's
only son, yet Jesus says of Zacchaeus, 'this man, too, is a son of
Abraham' (Luke 19:9).

Each person had their place in Jewish society, and
that place was God-ordained in the Law. There was an
understanding that vocations ran in families or tribes –

prophets were expected to be the sons of prophets; the Temple musicians belonged to the tribe of Levi – and family duty and commitment was central to what it meant to be a Jew. It is important to understand this societal character to grasp how radical were some of the things Jesus said.

When Jesus defended Mary at Bethany against her sister Martha's complaints (Luke 10:38–42), he was defending for a woman what might usually belong to a man – the privilege to study theology while the women busied themselves with the domestic routine. He breaks social tradition.

Mark's gospel records an occasion when Jesus was teaching in a mixed group of men and women. His family come to 'take charge of him' (section him) because he is rumoured to be out of his mind (Mark 3:21). They cannot get into the house because of the tight throng of people, and send word to him that they are there waiting to see him. He redefines what it means to belong when he replies: '"Who are my mother and my brothers?"... Then he looked at those seated in a circle around him and said, "Here are my mother and my brothers! Whoever does God's will is my brother and sister and mother"' (Mark 3:33–35).

The exciting and radical implication of his words is that belonging is a matter of choice, open to anyone. Family loyalties apply, but they are the loyalties of the family of faith rather than tribal loyalties. Into the household of faith that gathers around Jesus, the strong emphasis on unity and community continues, but it is determined not by birth but by the individual responsibility of personal choice.

The Old Testament as well as the New expects the accountability of the individual, but there is an immense difference in a community which is *created* by choice rather than by birth. Opting in is a different matter from opting out: but in the case of both kinds of community, belonging implies commitment.

Relationships open doorways, entry points and secret passageways into our souls. In the Old Testament, the People of God moved as one, their lives governed and bound by the Law. The Law created their boundary marker, and could be appealed to as an authority acknowledged by the whole People of God. If you were in that family, it applied to you.

In the New Testament, as the household of faith created by personal individual choice begins to form from peoples of varying religious and moral backgrounds, Paul recognizes the need to set boundaries, because as the Gentiles join the young church in large numbers, the Law can no longer offer a commonly acknowledged framework for life and belief in the same way it once did. So Paul urges caution and responsibility in making wise choices.

In an interesting passage from 2 Corinthians, he passionately defends the right of those who were excluded to belong, making it clear that though Christ's household of faith and Kingdom of grace are open to all, what is on offer is certainly not a life with no boundaries:

> Do not be yoked together with unbelievers. For what do
> righteousness and wickedness have in common? Or what
> fellowship can light have with darkness? What harmony
> is there between Christ and Belial? What does a believer
> have in common with an unbeliever? What agreement is
> there between the temple of God and idols? For we are the
> temple of the living God. As God has said: 'I will live with
> them and walk among them, and I will be their God, and
> they will be my people.'

'Therefore come out from them and be separate, says
the Lord. Touch no unclean thing, and I will receive you.'

'I will be a Father to you, and you will be my sons and
daughters, says the Lord Almighty.'

2 Corinthians 6:14–18

In his deliberations about marriage in 1 Corinthians 7, Paul
similarly urges caution – and for the same reason: because
once a person is married, their choices are thereafter inevitably
influenced, moderated and limited by the choices and
preferences of their spouse. This is true even when both persons
in a couple are believers. For example, if a believing man who
has been very responsible in his management of money marries
a believing woman who is absolutely clueless about financial
management, he will find himself yoked together with a life
practice that takes him places which give him cause for anxiety
and regret, however much he loves her – and which will tie up
his energies and time, that could have been better stewarded if
both had been wise and prudent people.

Our relationships create doorways in our boundaries: and
if we are unequally yoked with feckless, unreflective, indiscreet
or improvident people – whether by marriage, business or
friendship – the results of their choices will show up in our
lives as well as their own.

So Paul teaches us to be cautious in our choices and
decisions, balancing off the accountability that goes with
commitment and belonging against the necessity to set firm
boundaries, that safeguard our freedom and security, allowing
us scope to steward our time and resources for the building of
Christ's Kingdom and to live quiet and godly lives that are a
credit to our Lord.

In this, as in all things, there is a balance to be struck: wise caution should not retreat into suspicion, distrust, paranoia and fear. We have much to learn from all our neighbours on this earth, and God is always there to rescue and guide us. Jesus was not fussy about the company he kept, nor afraid of a tarnished reputation. Something we could learn from Jesus is the value of simplicity in defending purity and integrity. Because he had nothing in his hands, was born in poverty and lived in simplicity, those who came to him had nothing to gain but the blessing of his essential self.

No one can scam money off you or nick your stuff if you don't have a hoard of wealth and possessions to begin with: and if what we have is not tempting to thieves but is inexpensive and ordinary, it is less likely to be stolen and easy to replace, so we won't need a life weighed down with multiple locks and insurances. The more complicated we make our schedules and stash of possessions, the more complicated our relationships become: management of it all takes up time and energy, we become anxious and tired. If we learn at least a little of how to live like Jesus, simplicity and openness will allow things to reveal themselves, become plain, in our lives. If we are not full of artful games ourselves, then schemes and dodges will be more obvious to our eyes. Simplicity makes us clear-sighted.

Living simply extends the Kingdom of Hope. That's how I see it. You can't have hope without possibilities; and living simply encourages possibilities to grow. More time. More space. More money left over. So, more freedom to choose, and become the person I meant to be one day when I finally had the time.

When we live simply like this, we can afford to be

hospitable without risking our integrity. Romans chapter 14 teaches about this, starting with the open and generous words: 'Accept him whose faith is weak, without passing judgment on disputable matters' (Romans 14:1). As John Wimber said about being 'fishers of men', 'You have to catch 'em before you can clean 'em!'

We have grounds for absolute confidence in the power and victory of our Lord Jesus and, if we walk humbly and faithfully each day with him, we do not need to fear the sin or unbelief of others as if it were an infection. Blessing comes both from being mindful to walk in purity, and being trusting enough to be generous and welcoming.

Walking in the road of blessing is not about knowing incantations or special prayers or techniques. There is no religious mumbo-jumbo to it. It is about making practical choices in everyday living that reflect the wise teaching of the scriptures and the way things really are. It is the way of God, not the way of the flesh, that is natural.

Chapter Four

Stepping Stones on the Road of Blessing

There are four key areas to focus upon as we practise walking in the road of blessing:

- How we pray and praise.
- How we manage our money.
- Our capacity to accept responsibility.
- The acted prophecy of our lives.

How we pray and praise

Because we are made in the image of God and have his *ruach* in us; because we have the promise that whatever we ask in the Name of Jesus will be granted – we know confidently that prayer changes things.

When we have looked to see how and where God's Spirit is flowing, and ascertained the will of the Father, we can be sure that as we pray along with that our prayer will move mountains, reshaping the landscape of our lives. Prayer will (not 'might': *will*) make a difference to our health, our relationships, our vocations, our homes, our neighbourhoods, our finances, our state of mind – and anything else we care to put on the list, really. No matter how many years they pray, the power of God to answer prayer goes on astounding and thrilling the faithful in the exciting adventure that their lives become as they get in the habit of walking the road of blessing.

Our prayers, as we have considered already, should be *specific*, and should resonate in harmony with the way we are living our lives (if we want them positively answered).

After the death of my previous husband, a year and a day went by and I felt the time had come to look for a new life companion. I am not called to singleness; but I am very discriminating about the company I keep. I had no intention of hanging out in pubs and clubs looking for eligible men. That is not my idea of the way to find a partner. I laid the matter before the Lord. I made an altar, and wrote out carefully a very specific petition, detailing with precision the attributes of the husband I was asking for. Not one or two generalizations but a whole A4 page of closely typed specifics. I addressed my petition with serious and whole-hearted believing intent to the Lord, and laid it with confidence on the altar. That was at the end of August. In the middle of September, my present husband came into my life as a potential partner (we had known each other for many years, but in a more formal acquaintanceship). Not only did he fulfil in every detail the hopeful list I had laid before the Lord, but as I got to know him better I discovered that though I had known him for many years, I was mistaken about some aspects of his character: where I was mistaken, he resembled not my assumptions but my list.

God's plan for our lives includes stretch and challenge and change:

> So I went down to the potter's house, and I saw him working at the wheel. But the pot he was shaping from the clay was marred in his hands; so the potter formed it into another pot, shaping it as seemed best to him.
>
> Then the word of the Lord came to me: 'O house of

Israel, can I not do with you as this potter does?' declares
the Lord. 'Like clay in the hand of the potter, so are you in
my hand, O house of Israel...'

Jeremiah 18:3–6

God is not a cosmic slot machine for getting things. In making
my petition for a new life partner, I had already consulted and
listened to God, considered his call upon my life and thought
deeply about what I had been sent here to do. My prayer was
flowing his way.

But even then, he had lessons for me embedded in the
blessing. My husband and I are right for each other; but our
marriage has stretched and challenged us, brought us to know
some important home truths about ourselves, revised our
understanding where we were trapped in illusions, confronted
us with our shortcomings and shown us all kinds of things we
would rather have avoided seeing. Our way together has not
been an easy way: but the challenges are the right challenges,
because the partner is the right partner. It doesn't always feel
easy, but we know how we got to where we are, and it always
feels right.

Prayer is not mechanistic, and the Spirit does not jump
when we say 'jump'. God is sovereign, and free. Even so, when
we pray specifically and intentionally after earnestly seeking
God's will and looking to see how he is moving in a situation,
we can expect to see our prayers answered.

When we pray together, we should *agree* in our petition.
This matters. While a circumstance is still uncertain, still
hatching, it is unhelpful to have people of differing views
pronouncing over it, blowing it around in different directions
and hampering the flow of its development:

Again, I tell you that if two of you on earth agree about anything you ask for, it will be done for you by my Father in heaven. For where two or three come together in my name, there am I with them.

Matthew 18:19–20

If you are praying for something, keep it between yourself and the Lord unless you have prayer partners you can trust to get in the same directional flow as your prayer. Sceptics will not only undermine your own faith, their sceptical words will create whirlpools and contraflows, slowing up and messing up the results you are working towards, because they also are made in God's image and have the power of his *ruach* within them. If your prayer is in Spirit and in truth, it cannot ultimately be derailed, but it can be delayed and impeded.

I find it very helpful to write prayers down physically, and place them physically on a physical altar. It helps in focusing, so we can be clear about both the specifics and the agreement – everyone can sign the petition if it is a prayer where people are agreeing to pray together. It also affirms and encourages our faith: it's surprising how many things we pray for, then forget about – even important things; keeping a record of our prayers and revisiting them, having a 'thank you' pile with transfers from the 'please' pile as they are answered, is wonderfully up-building to our faith and confidence in God. When we look back with amazement at how often we see clear answers to our prayer, it helps us to persevere in prayer and to feel equanimity about our remaining puzzles and disappointments, trusting in the hand of God to lead us even where the way is unrevealed.

Praying the Word of God in the Bible is a wonderful way to experience the Spirit leading us forward in the way of blessing. My favourite way of all to do this is to attend Cathedral worship. As the choir chants the Psalms, the slow, measured singing helps me to abide deeply in the sacred words, lingering in the ancient and inspired prayers, touching the presence of God, encountering his living Word for me, for my day, in the holy Scripture. Such dwelling on the Word of God in prayer allows me to confront truths I had been avoiding, heals me, speaks to me. Others like to pray the Scriptures in daily Bible reading notes that help them to focus on a particular verse or passage, and loiter with intent on the corner of the street where God's majesty will pass by.

Praise is at least as powerful to effect change as prayer, especially when we are praying about something internal – our mood, our health, our faith, our attitude. In times of confusion, depression and sadness, moments when we have lost our way and cannot see the path ahead, praise can get us back onto the road of blessing.

My dear friend Margery, who taught me so much and often is mentioned in my writing, used to employ praise to haul herself out of the pit. She lived in the seaside town of Hastings, and was a widow for several decades. Sometimes she felt very lonely and vulnerable, and at such times could rapidly slide into a very low mood indeed, when life's struggles and problems began to seem insurmountable. When that happened, she would go for a walk beside the ocean. Whatever the weather, in sunshine, rain, wind or storm, she would stride all the way along the three miles of Hastings promenade and back, praising God for absolutely everything in her life. She praised him for her home and her family, for the privilege of knowing Jesus personally, for the gifts of the Holy Spirit, for her brothers and sisters in Christ, for the opportunity of being a Christian artist, for the ministry of healing, for the Word of God in the Bible, for the wild waves of the sea and the flight of the gulls, for the strength of her legs to walk, for the chance to be married and have children, for the lessons learned in living through two world wars, for the beauty of the hills and the clouds, for her salvation in Christ, for the need to turn to God in prayer… everything. By the time she had completed her walk, without fail her spirits were lifted and the demons that plagued her had been chased away.

Praise changes us. I cannot now recall which Christian writer challenged us, 'Are you prayed-up and praised-up?' but it is a wise check to make. The person who meets the day standing on the promises of God, having committed his or her way to the Lord and praised his holy Name for every circumstance, rests in strength. Life is different, when we remember to pray and to praise. People who walk in praise walk in blessing.

How we manage our money

This is so important. If we are not managing our money according to the Word of God in the scriptures, then we will not be able to walk in the road of blessing.

It is quite possible for people who are not familiar with the Bible to manage their money in such a way as to attract blessing and follow the road of blessing: these principles of money management are not true because they're in the Bible, they're in the Bible because they're true. However we come by these truths, they're still true. This is the way life works, because all life proceeds from God and this is the way God works. Here is what the Bible teaches about how to manage our money:

Stay out of debt

> Give everyone what you owe him: If you owe taxes, pay
> taxes; if revenue, then revenue; if respect, then respect; if
> honour, then honour. Let no debt remain outstanding,
> except the continuing debt to love one another, for he who
> loves his fellow-man has fulfilled the law.
>
> *Romans 13:7–8*

This text makes clear that we should be honourable with our money, paying our bills and paying our taxes, never seeking to cheat or evade payment of what is due from us.

Our lives should be free of debt. Freedom from debt is not an end in itself simply, but is the gateway to other forms of freedom. If the Lord calls us on to a new task or mission, it is our responsibility to be ready to obey his word to us. Debts keep us stuck where we are, and slow down massively our ability to respond and move on.

Debts also tie us tightly into the reign of Mammon, as our interest payments support and finance the ways of the world. If we are faithful to Christ's desire that we be 'in the world but not of the world' (see 1 John 2:15–17; John 15:19; 17), we shall not allow ourselves to be drawn into this entanglement.

This way of living means that if we have a credit card, we must see to it that we pay it off in full each month, that we create a savings buffer to dip into rather than a bank overdraft, that we save for what we need rather than taking the hire-purchase route.

Debt is foundational to the way our society works, and to avoid debt is distinctly counter-cultural. It is normal for accommodation to be acquired through mortgage debt, and education to be financed by student loans. This is not the way of blessing. Sometimes, even for believers, a mortgage and a student loan are chosen because they seem to be the only practical option. If we have chosen that, we should not add to the burden of the debt a matching burden of guilt – that is not helpful at all. We live with our choices and we bear our burdens serenely: but if we ever get the chance, we should free ourselves immediately from those burdens of debt; they keep us chained to Mammon, and they are not a source of blessing. If we doubt that, we need only ask ourselves, 'Does this mortgage increase or decrease my freedom?' A mortgage ties us up for many years; we become the bond-slave of the mortgage lender.

The way of the Spirit, the way of blessing, is a way of freedom (John 8:32, 36). It's also true, of course, that education and owning our own home are helpful in creating stability and security in our lives: so we should not be downhearted if we have chosen a mortgage or student loan as a means of establishing security – that can be a responsible choice. But it's wise to hold in mind that a loan is a second-best choice: best of all is freedom; and watching and praying for the chance to be free is part of walking the road of blessing.

We help ourselves if we choose what is humble and frugal, and if we are willing to accept the compromises and sacrifices of sharing with others. Then it is far easier to avoid the chains and obligations of debt, and to walk as free people in the world.

I have always loved this Scripture from Deuteronomy, which seems to me to express how the track of blessing passes unobtrusively and quietly through the world:

From the desert of Kedemoth I sent messengers to Sihon
king of Heshbon offering peace and saying, 'Let us pass
through your country. We will stay on the main road; we
will not turn aside to the right or to the left. Sell us food
to eat and water to drink for their price in silver. Only let
us pass through on foot – as the descendants of Esau, who
live in Seir, and the Moabites, who live in Ar, did for us –
until we cross the Jordan into the land the Lord our God
is giving us.'

Deuteronomy 2:26–29

The world is not our home; we are only passing through. We
who are believers accept the discipline of freedom, the discipline
of the pilgrim travelling light. The pilgrim knows that debts
of every kind bind us to a place, subtly and inescapably tying
us down. The road of blessing is a free and living way: debts
have no part in it.

Release others from debt

The Lord's Prayer (Matthew 6:9–13; Luke 11:2–4) speaks
about forgiveness. What is not clear, because the two texts
differ, is whether Jesus meant that we were to release others
from the moral obligation of sin, or whether we should also
release them from the obligation of financial debt.

We have to be practical about this. Sometimes it will be
very helpful and kind to lend somebody money; and when
we do, sometimes, especially if they have been used to a
very chaotic lifestyle, it may be good for them to accept the
discipline of paying the money back.

This principle of releasing others from debt, like the

119

principle of not getting into debt ourselves, is exactly that – a *principle*: not a dogmatic encumbrance that of itself curtails our freedom. We are talking not about nit-picking legalism, but about a generous and forgiving management of money, that tempers the wind to the shorn lamb, and supports both discipline and freedom.

Jesus said (Luke 4:16–21) that his coming fulfilled the foretelling of the one who would proclaim the 'year of the Lord's favour', the Jubilee year in which slaves were set free and debts were forgiven. 'The Way', as Christian discipleship was known in its early days, brought good news for the poor (and for the rich as well) because it increased hope and security and freedom, reducing drudgery and misery and regret.

The Way of Christ embraces the principle of grace that allows everyone who needs it a fresh start. It is founded on the belief that, because life is spiritual and originates with God who is full of loving-kindness, we will see miracles of provision as we abandon ourselves to divine providence, walking in trust not fear.

The teaching of the whole Bible supports this approach to money management, calling us to extend mercy towards one another's difficulty and need:

> If you lend money to one of my people among you
> who is needy, do not be like a money-lender; charge
> him no interest. If you take your neighbour's cloak as a
> pledge, return it to him by sunset, because his cloak is
> the only covering he has for his body. What else will he
> sleep in? When he cries out to me, I will hear, for I am
> compassionate.
>
> *Exodus 22:25–27*

120

We are called to live simply, humbly and frugally, free of debt: and generously, kindly and mercifully, offering the help others need to join us on the way of freedom.

As we practise this way, we have in mind Jesus' teaching that we are to be as 'wily as dragons and as innocent as doves' (Matthew 10:16, my paraphrase): our kindness to others should not be a collusion with profligate ways, we are not to become the dupes of opportunists or stupidly naive.

Jesus was protected against opportunists by his choice of radical simplicity, and we can learn from him for our own lives. If we are satisfied with humble, low-status belongings and ourselves walk the way of simplicity, what we have to offer will be less attractive to predatory people. And when our friends who manage money ineptly find themselves in trouble one more time, sometimes the best way to help is to show them what they can do to solve the problem on their own. We were not sent into the world to be the sugar daddies of the whole human race, but to set an example that others could follow so their lives would be healed.

Do not practise usury

Recent economic history should be enough to illustrate the wisdom of this principle, and the biblical texts in support of it are numerous. Nehemiah 5 has an interesting story that deals with the subject of usury, and the books of the Law in the Old Testament are very clear about it.

The teaching of the Old Testament Law, however, that interest must not be charged on loans, applies not to every loan but only to loans to fellow Jews: to charge a Gentile interest was permissible:

> Do not charge your brother interest, whether on money
> or food or anything else that may earn interest. You may
> charge a foreigner interest, but not a brother Israelite, so
> that the Lord your God may bless you in everything you
> put your hand to in the land you are entering to possess.
>
> *Deuteronomy 23:19–20*

This aspect of the Law makes clear the connection between blessing and abstaining from usury. The prohibition on charging interest on a loan made to a fellow Jew, while permitting interest on loans to Gentiles, is of great interest and significance. The ancient Jews were a warrior race, and other races were usually seen as competitors. The rules for living in the Law are intended to safeguard and build up the community. Usury is clearly being identified as something which erodes the strength of a community, which drags it down – so by all means charge interest on loans to people you want to weaken or undermine, but never demand interest payments of those you want to strengthen and consolidate.

So we ask ourselves these questions: Whom do we wish to strengthen? Whom do we wish to weaken and undermine? For the ancient Jews, the answer was simple – they wanted to weaken and undermine everyone who was not them. They understood God to be a tribal God, a God who had their interests (and nobody else's) at heart. But Jesus expanded our ideas of God, and expanded our ideas about belonging:

> A crowd was sitting around him, and they told him, 'Your
> mother and brothers are outside looking for you.'
>
> 'Who are my mother and my brothers?' he asked.
>
> Then he looked at those seated in a circle around him

and said, 'Here are my mother and my brothers! Whoever
does God's will is my brother and sister and mother.'

Mark 3:32–35

Christ's household, his tribe, his holy nation, is formed by
choice and by adoption through grace, not by race and birth.
So the 'brother' to whom we must not lend money at interest
is potentially *anyone*! Not just church members – anyone:
because it would be unworkable to set up a moneylender's
outfit charged with identifying which applicants were and
were not 'doing God's will'.

Christ's Kingdom of grace sets us free from the legalism
and constraints of the Law – but its discipline is no less
demanding. When Christ said that we were called to walk in a
'strait and narrow way', he wasn't joking! 'Because strait is the
gate, and narrow is the way, which leadeth unto life, and few
there be that find it' (Matthew 7:14 KJV). Indeed, there are
few that find it, because the cost is considerable, even though
it is a way of freedom, grace and unbelievable joy.

It is odd that the church has been so loud in its
condemnation of homosexuality, which affects maybe ten per
cent in any population, and so silent about the practice of
usury, which affects every individual with a savings account,
a credit card, a student loan, a mortgage, a hire purchase
agreement or an overdraft. The entire economic structure of
our society is built upon usury.

The road of blessing leads us out of usury. Because we
are in the world, members of society, it is impossible to be free
of it. Just as we can choose to eat a healthy diet, avoid drugs
and alcohol and promiscuity, get enough rest and exercise –
but still be at risk from pollutants and traffic accidents and

burglary because we live where we do, so we cannot disengage ourselves entirely from the Mammon-tangle our society has got itself into. But at least we can understand it: we can be clear about what the Bible teaches and, so far as it is practically possible for us, put it into practice in our lives. We bear in mind that the road of blessing is directional and intentional – it is about journey, not stasis. We shall not get there all at once; but we need to be clear about where we are heading, and set our course by that star.

For example, our choice to keep out of debt will already have reduced our involvement with usury because (if we have borrowed at all) we shall have borrowed the minimum and will be making the least possible interest payments in our household budget. If we have money to invest, we might choose to buy a house or flat and let it to tenants: as fair and thoughtful landlords we would bless their lives, and we would avoid the option to increase our wealth by interest gained from bank investments.

And how many of us, after all, enquire with care into how and where our money is invested? In guns and bombs? In sweatshop factories? There are a few savings banks that place our investments only in projects that benefit the community (my favourite is the Triodos Bank) – but these organizations are a tiny minority, and most Christians have their savings lodged with high street banks.

Because our whole society is founded on usury (the reign of Mammon is that deeply entrenched), it is almost impossible to shake free of it. Few of us can handle our affairs without involvement with banks and bank practices. We can do only what is practically possible: but we bear in mind it is the *direction* that matters. Step by step, we travel in the direction of blessing: away from usury – for ourselves, for our families, for our neighbours, for our nation, for our world. Wherever we have influence and choice, we opt to avoid usury, and to avoid debt. As circumstances are now, we may not immediately achieve perfection; but the Lord will see which way we are walking.

> Lord, who may dwell in your sanctuary?
> Who may live on your holy hill?
> He whose walk is blameless
> and who does what is righteous,
> who speaks the truth from his heart
> and has no slander on his tongue,
> who does his neighbour no wrong
> and casts no slur on his fellow-man,
> who despises a vile man
> but honours those who fear the Lord,
> who keeps his oath
> even when it hurts,
> who lends his money without usury
> and does not accept a bribe against the innocent.
> He who does these things
> will never be shaken.
>
> *Psalm 15:1–5*

Be generous in giving

Many Christians adopt the Old Testament rule of paying to the Lord a tithe (ten per cent) of all they earn: and those who practise this invariably testify that the nine-tenths go further than the whole. When they give to the Lord, they find themselves on the road of blessing. Others see tithing as just a start, the basic minimum, and would argue that as wealth increases, so should the proportion that is given away.

Some low-income families feel unable to manage the tithe. For them, it is not possible to work out a budget: by the time the rent and utilities, the essential insurances and transport and food are subtracted, the budget has already ceased to work on paper – there is nothing to take a tithe from. They are already trusting in the Lord for his provision. So it seems to me that it is not wise to be legalistic about tithing, though it is a wise rule of thumb to guide us in our giving.

But the principle of the road of blessing is generosity. Some months, we may have nothing spare and be resting on the Lord's provision. Other times we may have a windfall and choose to use it all to help somebody who is struggling. At all times we will be ready with hospitality and kindness, looking to see where we can contribute, what we have to offer and how we can help. This is the way of blessing.

Though the Old Testament rule about tithing creates blessing, the New Testament ideas about giving and sharing take us on beyond that rule, just as we saw the ideas about who is our community expanded as we moved from the Old Testament to the New.

> They devoted themselves to the apostles' teaching and to
> the fellowship, to the breaking of bread and to prayer.
> Everyone was filled with awe, and many wonders and
> miraculous signs were done by the apostles. All the
> believers were together and had everything in common.
> Selling their possessions and goods, they gave to anyone as
> he had need. Every day they continued to meet together

in the temple courts. They broke bread in their homes and
ate together with glad and sincere hearts, praising God
and enjoying the favour of all the people. And the Lord
added to their number daily those who were being saved.

Acts 2:42–47

This passage from the book of Acts offers us a vision of a community in which the tithe has become unnecessary – because *everything* is given, *everything* is shared.

The Old Testament rule of tithing tends to enhance our sense of boundaries, giving us a very clear awareness of what is our own, from which we must calculate and donate a tenth. But the New Testament principle of sharing carries the concept of giving beyond the tenth to a hundred per cent: whole-hearted community, whole-hearted unity, sharing life and food and goods and possessions. It makes me feel exhausted just thinking about it! The only way it could not be too costly is if the whole project was fuelled by joy, by the exhilaration of God's Spirit welling up in the hearts of the people.

Where does that leave us? Think about the people in your church. Do you trust them? Do you want to live with them, eat supper with them every day, share a bank account? Possibly not. There are, of course, many Christian communities – monastic or Anabaptist or other intentional communities – who do live out the faith in this way. Yet even in those first heady days of the church, as we read the epistles and the book of Acts carefully, we see that Christians did still live in normal households: only, the barriers of fear and suspicion seem to have been blown right away.

The road of blessing is a way of openness and generosity rather than a system of rules and conditions to be met. Tithing is an excellent practice; but you don't have to tithe to join the road of blessing. Tithing or not tithing, what takes you onto the road of blessing is swift and compassionate generosity, kind hospitality; the love that shelters those in trouble and lifts up the weak. 'Each man should give what he has decided in his heart to give, not reluctantly or under compulsion, for God loves a cheerful giver' (2 Corinthians 9:7).

Take care of your family

> If anyone does not provide for his relatives, and especially
> for his immediate family, he has denied the faith and is
> worse than an unbeliever.
>
> *1 Timothy 5:8*

Many who feel called to Christian ministry fall into the trap of neglecting their families, and all feel the tension of trying to balance family time against the hungry demands of ministry. Few of those who are zealous in the practice of their faith see their children wishing to follow in their footsteps. Paul asks this question: 'If anyone does not know how to manage his own family, how can he take care of God's church?' (1 Timothy 3:5).

I have never really understood the concept of the supernatural, for it seems to me that everything is natural. God made the universe and everything in it, so all things that are and the *way* things are, are both entirely natural and entirely God-blessed and God-breathed. Therefore what is natural will speak to us of God and lead us into blessing. So I take seriously the things that occur naturally in my life; and the most important of those things is my family.

128

In the preaching and teaching ministry of the church, and in the literature of aid organizations, we are reminded often of Jesus' exhortation from the Law to love our neighbours as ourselves (Mark 12:31; see also Leviticus 19:18). Both the glory and the challenge of the Gospel centre in its lowering of barriers and blurring of distinctions. In Luke's gospel, a teacher of the Law discussing these matters with Jesus (Luke 10:29) and wanting to justify himself, asked him: 'And who is my neighbour?' The story of the Good Samaritan that Jesus tells in response makes it clear that the term 'neighbour' may include the person I hate and despise, the person I cross the street to avoid, the person I want nothing to do with at all.

From this, preachers have often taken the inference that to the question: 'And who is my neighbour?' the answer should be – 'Everyone!' That is a magnificent vision, but it has limitations when it comes to practical application. Interestingly, the same question has been asked in Islam with a very careful and exact answer, specifying that my neighbours are those who live within the bounds of forty houses' distance from mine in every direction. Could I love all those people? At a stretch, possibly. Could I love everyone? No.

It seems to me that the parable of the Good Samaritan teaches us not to love *everyone* but to love *anyone*. In the story, the good man showed love towards the person he came across. If he had tried to love the whole world, he would have run out of money, time and energy in the shortest order. He loved the person God sent his way – *whoever that might be*. And I think that is what God is asking us to do. The most immediate of those he has sent our way must surely be our families. He has entrusted them to us, to act in their best interest, to pray for them, shelter them, encourage and strengthen them, and to show them by all means in our power the way of grace.

In the use of our money, the first call of our stewardship is in the provision for the needs and benefits of those God has entrusted into our care. A society which believed and acted upon such a concept would be far stronger and freer, far safer and happier, than the Mammon-sprawl of modern life. Even the church is affected by the ways of Mammon. I met an elderly lady, a faithful church member, afflicted by arthritis. She needed her home adapting to take account of her increasing disability. She told me that her son, a prominent churchgoer and a well-to-do banker, was being a wonderful help to her in this matter. I assumed she meant he was fixing her home appliances, but no. His help consisted in assisting her with filling out complex application forms to seek financial help from the government, as she herself was poor. I can imagine he made a very good banker, but his chosen approach was not the road of blessing: 'There were no needy persons among them' (Acts 4:34). If we wish to walk in the way of blessing, we will take care of the people who belong to us ourselves, so far as our means allow.

The handling of our finances should be determined (along with everything else in our lives) by the imperatives of love and responsibility. Loving our neighbour is entwined with managing our money: and our neighbour is the person God has put in our path; and whoever else that includes, it includes our family.

Leave something for the gleaner

The practice of tithing, taken from the Old Testament, has clear and articulate advocates in the church, but not the other Old Testament injunction of leaving something for the gleaner:

> When you reap the harvest of your land, do not reap to
> the very edges of your field or gather the gleanings of your
> harvest. Leave them for the poor and the alien. I am the
> Lord your God.
>
> *Leviticus 23:22*

> Woe to you who add house to house and join field to field
> till no space is left and you live alone in the land.
>
> *Isaiah 5:8*

> He replied, 'It is not right to take the children's bread and
> toss it to their dogs.'
>   'Yes, Lord,' she said, 'but even the dogs eat the crumbs
> that fall from their masters' table.'
>
> *Matthew 15:26–27*

People everywhere who live on the margins rely on gleaning in one form or another to survive. People who are poor and marginalized can get by on very little, often ask for almost nothing, and do not expect much from life at all. They live in tiny dwellings and on patches of rough land on the edge of town. They make do with cast-offs and hand-me-downs, and what others throw away. They are resourceful, but they do need something to be resourceful with.

It is a mistake to think that this robs the poor of dignity. Poverty is relative, but for sizeable periods of my life I have been what many would consider to be poor. Sometimes I have waited at the market at the end of the day to pick up the vegetables dropped or thrown out when the stall-holders left. When my children were young, I waited until the end of the school year when the lost property was displayed and any unclaimed items were moved on: that was where we got our children's winter coats – some wealthier children didn't like the ones their parents had chosen and 'lost' them on purpose. I've burned firewood gathered in the hedgerow (dead wood fallen, not torn from a growing tree) and fir cones picked up on the street, and junk mail and cardboard packaging, to keep warm. Doing this felt triumphant – the wolf from the door successfully beaten back!

I glean in the lean times, and when times are easier, I leave something over for the gleaners. When we moved from our house in Aylesbury which we shared with lodgers, to share a house with other members of our family in Hastings, we knew our lodgers' bedroom furniture would be surplus. Meanwhile a neighbour was preparing to let rooms in his home. He was not a rich man. When we gave him our surplus furniture, he was overjoyed, could hardly believe it – that we would just give it to him. But the money we could save him far exceeded the money we could raise by selling it – so it made good sense. Good sense, that is, once we realize that we all belong to one another, that our neighbour is sent us by God to look out for, to encourage, to help along.

The wonderful Freecycle network has been a blessing to all gleaners and edge-dwellers: surplus belongings or requests for wants are posted on the Freecycle website for your local area; and those who have things they don't want are matched with those looking for something they lack. No money changes hands.

As long as the children let the crumbs fall from the table for the dogs to catch, everyone can get by somehow.

It is when people get greedy, when they want to take not only something but everything: when they over-fish the oceans until the fish stocks collapse and the species that depend on fish for food are threatened; when farmers have been persuaded to buy GM hybrid seeds (seeds that cannot be saved) and their accompanying necessary pesticides, so the farmer as well as his money is in the pocket of the manufacturer; when saving and sharing seed is seen as theft of intellectual property, because patents (like that on basmati rice) have been granted; when rainforests are cut down and tribal peoples dispossessed to make room for the cattle ranches and oil-palm groves of giant corporations – when this happens, and there is no margin left for the gleaner, people become desperate, human society unravels, the seeds of war are sown, and our feet have left the way of blessing for the swamps and pits of the wilderness. 'Do not go over your vineyard a second time or pick up the grapes that have fallen. Leave them for the poor and the alien. I am the Lord your God' (Leviticus 19:10).

Practise hospitality

> Share with God's people who are in need. Practise hospitality.
>
> *Romans 12:13*

> Offer hospitality to one another without grumbling.
>
> *1 Peter 4:9*

> Come, you who are blessed by my Father; take your inheritance, the kingdom prepared for you since the creation of the world. For I was hungry and you gave me

something to eat, I was thirsty and you gave me something
to drink, I was a stranger and you invited me in…

Matthew 25:34–35

The alien living with you must be treated as one of your
native-born. Love him as yourself, for you were aliens in
Egypt. I am the Lord your God.

Leviticus 19:34

God setteth the solitary in families…

Psalm 68:6 KJV

As we walk the way of blessing, sooner or later our feet will take
us through a place where we are asked to care for the lonely and
the stranger. As we learn to share and build community, our
homes become safe, welcoming, happy places where people
want to come who are lost and have no one.

My mother's mantra, by which she has lived her life, is:
'The important thing is to both maintain and progress.' She's
right. If we lose what we have achieved by the gains we make,
then we will never go forward. If we are content to stay where
we are and let things slide, equally we shall never go forward.
The task in life is to maintain the good we have achieved, while
working to progress on to greater things.

This principle can be applied, with great benefit, to
our thinking about hospitality. Hospitality is one of the
gentle virtues, a lovely grace that should be evident in each
Christian life. But hospitality without caution and due regard
to boundaries creates mayhem.

Each household has a dynamic of its own, a delicate
balance of relationships continually renegotiated as the

individuals who live together develop and change in the course of life. Every person who is introduced into the household, or who feels free to call there uninvited, will alter the current dynamic of the home and family. This may be especially true of troubled individuals or people who have suffered deep trauma. The soul, the power, of their trouble and suffering will radiate from them to affect the home and all its members. Therefore, for the well-being of those who live there, and for the peace and security of the home, it is important to consider prayerfully and in consultation with the other members of the household before opening their home too enthusiastically to people in trouble.

All of us can and should help people in trouble, and some people have that beautiful ministry of hospitality which allows them to run an open house so calm and healing and loving that troubled souls find their way to harmony just by being there.

When I was a teenager, I was privileged to come across just such a household. The mother and father were full of loving-kindness and holy wisdom. Two of their seven children were adopted, and any day of the week you could expect to find the mother of that home sitting peacefully at her fireside darning socks, listening to the troubles of an endless stream of people who called in to her house. A comfy chair and a cup of tea was offered to everyone who called. It was one of the sanest, most creative homes I have ever come across.

When I was a young mother, my path took me through a time when I had much to do with prison ministry and people in distress. My children grew up in a small house where people with intractable mental illness, convicts on leave and ex-convicts needing a place to stay, were frequent visitors. The children saw for themselves at first hand what wreckage drugs and alcohol can make of a quite ordinary person's life: saw that even people who look quite frightening on the street can be loving friends; but also lived through the experiences of alarming encounters with unstable individuals, and having their purses stolen, and opening the door to find the police on the step with some questions to ask.

As children, they took it all in their stride. Later on, when their father left us and we lost our home and income, it became important to focus on re-establishing trust in life and a sense of security: so I became more cautious about who came into our home. We ourselves were broken and afraid; for a long while we needed our home base to be a very private place where we could be comforted and healed.

But even in that private place, a group of friends began to gather: single women who were trustworthy and respectable, but who had themselves been abandoned, or who were without family of their own. So a different kind of hospitality began to emerge, a mutually supportive group of women, who separately were vulnerable and anxious, but together found laughter, strength and confidence. I listened in my living room to the woman who ten years ago had stood at a bus stop with ten pounds in her pocket and a child (one disabled) holding each hand, wondering where to go and what to do; I reassured the woman whose husband had just told her he had found someone new and wanted to sell their home immediately, that she would come through this, she would be happy again one day, it would be okay in the end.

It is important to practise hospitality, to open our homes and friendship to the lonely and distressed and those who are drawn to that space; but it is just as important to be shrewd in our judgment, to apply common sense in our choices. The hospitality that is appropriate for us to offer at one stage of life will not be suitable in another. Every Christian is called to create a welcoming, hospitable home; but keeping in mind the security and peace and well-being of the people who already live there. If there are desperate people whom for the moment we feel unable to help, then we owe it to them to hold them in God's love in prayer, and to support in those ways that we can manage the foundations and organizations that work to help them. This is the way of blessing.

'Do not forget to entertain strangers, for by so doing some people have entertained angels without knowing it' (Hebrews 13:2). In offering hospitality we do indeed entertain angels unawares: you have to open the shutters to let the sunshine in.

Do not worry about anything but cast your cares upon God

Do not be anxious about anything, but in everything,
by prayer and petition, with thanksgiving, present your
requests to God. And the peace of God, which transcends
all understanding, will guard your hearts and your minds
in Christ Jesus.

Philippians 4:6–7

Cast all your anxiety on him because he cares for you.
1 Peter 5:7

Ask and it will be given to you; seek and you will find;
knock and the door will be opened to you.
Matthew 7:7

Therefore I tell you, do not worry about your life... So do not worry... Therefore do not worry...

Matthew 6:25, 31, 34

He who did not spare his own Son, but gave him up for us all – how will he not also, along with him, graciously give us all things?

Romans 8:32

But seek first his kingdom and his righteousness, and all these things will be given to you as well.

Matthew 6:33

I am not sure quite how this works, but people tend to attract what is on their minds. What we focus upon in our thinking will grow in our lives. This doesn't apply only to the things we desire and yearn for, but also to the things we worry about and dread.

How do people communicate? My twins have a memory of sitting in their pram, discussing how best to get out. It was too far to climb down; they needed someone to help them. They tried calling out to their oldest sister, but she disappointingly paid no heed to their SOS. They called to their second sister when she came into the garden, and she came over to speak to them. They explained the problem, and she ran off to find an adult who would lift them safely down.

The really interesting feature of those conversations becomes apparent when you realize that our twins outgrew that pram when they were six months old, and were no longer left sitting in it after that. So their discussion with each other and explanation to their sister took place before they were able to speak. A very chatty family of children born close together in age (I had five babies in six years) has resulted in memories being not buried or lost but perpetuated and discussed: my children have several memories of their journey into speech and the time that came before they took that momentous human step.

What becomes clear from these recollections is that people can call out to each other, and broadcast intention, on a sub-verbal (i.e. telepathic) level. Sometimes Christians are uneasy with telepathy, fearing it as an occult phenomenon: personally I believe it to be a natural occurrence that is part of everyone's life. I think that, at a level underlying conscious awareness, we are broadcasting our attitudes, hopes, dreams, prejudices, anxieties and fears, all the time, to each other and the rest of creation. And as we send out consistent thought signals (we, who are made in the image of creator God), so we command the natural order to organize faithfully according to our view of life. We call into being both what we long for and what we fear – whatever it is that we concentrate sustainedly upon, and what we really believe.

So it is not merely a good idea but absolutely crucial that we do not worry about anything, but cast all our cares upon God. As we focus our thinking upon him, walking trustingly and steadily in the light of his overshining love, blessed by the light of his countenance bending over us – what shall we lack? Of what shall we be afraid?

Walking this way, we create a track of blessing, as our habits of mind broadcast our confidence and faith, and we begin to see blessing made manifest, according to our firm belief.

Our thoughts make things happen. It is well for our thoughts to be fixed on God and his good purposes.

The beautiful words of Psalm 27:1–6 (here from the KJV) make a wonderful declaration of power and intent at times when we feel tempted to be afraid, when we are almost overwhelmed:

> The Lord is my light and my salvation; whom shall I fear? The Lord is the strength of my life; of whom shall I be afraid?
>
> When the wicked, even mine enemies and my foes, came upon me to eat up my flesh, they stumbled and fell.
>
> Though an host should encamp against me, my heart shall not fear: though war should rise against me, in this will I be confident.
>
> One thing have I desired of the Lord, that will I seek after; that I may dwell in the house of the Lord all the days of my life, to behold the beauty of the Lord, and to enquire in his temple.
>
> For in the time of trouble he shall hide me in his pavilion: in the secret of his tabernacle shall he hide me; he shall set me up upon a rock.
>
> And now shall mine head be lifted up above mine enemies round about me: therefore will I offer in his tabernacle sacrifices of joy; I will sing, yea, I will sing praises unto the Lord.

Pray for what you need, and seek first the Kingdom

We have already looked carefully in this chapter at how prayer and praise both affect and effect our experience of blessing: there is no need to go over the same ground. Even so, in this section about our experience of blessing being influenced by how we manage our money, the habit of prayer should have another mention.

You, like me, will have met many Sunday Christians – believers who sit there in chapel at worship, joining in with the prayers with head bowed. 'Mmm, yes, Lord! Hallelujah, Lord! Yes, Father! Amen!' they murmur, just loud enough for everyone to hear. And on Monday morning they go back to sharp practice at work, speaking ill of colleagues, ruthless in business, selfish in their ways and domineering at home. This is not how we get the Kingdom built, and it is the Kingdom that will keep us all happy and safe and secure. If we want to be happy and safe in our everyday lives, we have to build the shelter, build the Kingdom – and we do that by our actual habits of speech and behaviour.

Money is useful – I was going to say 'we all need money', but actually that isn't true. Some people (Peace Pilgrim, for example; you can read about her on the internet) have created a way of life in which they do not rely on money as most of us do, and I admire them. Even so, money is useful, and most of us depend upon it. But money is not our principal currency – rather, faith is – and that depends on God's loving kindness and provision for our lives. It is as we trust him and lean upon his providence, as we commit all things to him in prayer, that we see our needs amazingly met. This is not to say that the lives of the faithful will be smooth and easy, without hardship – ask any Christians you know, and that'll bring a smile to their faces! It's that as we trust God and focus upon him, humbly seek his help and commit our way to him in prayer, then even in the midst of hardship we are upheld and our needs are met.

If we try to manage our money without prayer and humility before God, we shall 'sow the wind and reap the whirlwind' (Hosea 8:7): if our feet are shod with the Gospel of peace, if we are walking in prayer, we shall be walking in blessing.

This is for even the detail of our lives, not just big investments and major decisions. When we go browsing in the mall, or out to do our Christmas shopping, we whisper in our hearts, 'Come with me, Lord: by your sweet Spirit influence my choices and decisions, what I purchase and what I leave behind.' When we look for T-shirts for the baby on eBay, we ask silently, 'This one, Father? This one? Tell me when I've spent enough.' And he is gracious: he involves himself in our littleness; we walk in the way of blessing, tightly holding his hand.

> Blessed is the man who does not walk in the counsel of the wicked or stand in the way of sinners or sit in the seat of mockers.
> But his delight is in the law of the Lord, and on his law he meditates day and night.
> He is like a tree planted by streams of water, which yields its fruit in season and whose leaf does not wither.
> Whatever he does prospers.
>
> *Psalm 1:1–3*

Our capacity to accept responsibility

> The man said, 'The woman you put here with me – she gave me some fruit from the tree, and I ate it.'
> Then the Lord God said to the woman, 'What is this you have done?'
> The woman said, 'The serpent deceived me, and I ate.'
>
> *Genesis 3:12–13*

Then the Lord said to Cain, 'Where is your brother Abel?'

142

'I don't know,' he replied. 'Am I my brother's keeper?'

The Lord said, 'What have you done? Listen! Your brother's blood cries out to me from the ground.'

Genesis 4:9–10

Each one should test his own actions. Then he can take pride in himself, without comparing himself to somebody else, for each one should carry his own load.

Galatians 6:4–5

Those who belong to Christ Jesus have crucified the sinful nature with its passions and desires. Since we live by the Spirit, let us keep in step with the Spirit.

Galatians 5:24–25

There are some things more clearly seen by their absence than by their presence. I remember once hearing a discussion among atheists and Christians, trying to establish some common ground in terms of world-view and belief structures. They had objections to almost everything each other thought, it seemed: but they did finally manage to agree on this – child abuse is always, without exception, regardless of circumstances, totally wrong.

I was fascinated to observe them thus inching towards understanding, finding a small overlap in their thinking in this negative: *abuse – wrong*. They were unable to agree entirely on what was right, or what was good for children: but they all thought child abuse was unequivocally wrong.

In the same way, it is not always easy to appreciate light without darkness. How beautiful are the stars; it is the contrast that makes them so poignantly and sublimely lovely. How beautiful is the dawn; and the spring. How welcome is a friend with a torch when you've lost your earring in a country lane at half past ten at night in the middle of November.

Responsibility is one of those things more clearly appreciated by its absence. Responsible people are often seen as killjoys, uncool; boring. You know the kind of people I mean? You toss your chocolate wrapper in the gutter and they stop and pick it up, and hand it back to you. You brag a little about the fab online poker game you played last night, where every time you lost you had to toss back a shot glass of vodka and you all passed out paralytic at one in the morning – and they don't think it's funny at all. Or you're really pleased to have found a supermarket where you can get a hot chicken for less than £3 – and they ask you what farming conditions made that kind of price possible.

Responsible people: they can be such a bore, can't they? Boring – until they are gone: and all you are left with is the cool dudes having a laugh who drove home drunk with your daughter in the passenger seat (may she rest in peace). Until all you are left with are the hip cats who like a little wacky baccy and a few pills to make the party go with a swing – and burgled your house to finance their habit.

A friend of mine pulled up at a busy junction and the motorist behind stopped too late and pranged his car. They got out, but the man behind suggested to my friend that they pull off the road round the corner to exchange insurance details, as they were holding up the traffic. My friend thought that seemed sensible and got back in his car, turned the corner and pulled off the road. He looked up in time to see the man who had pranged his car driving away laughing at him.

When I was a child, the buses in Yorkshire all had signs saying 'No Spitting'. Encouraging people to stop spitting on the street and on the floor of the bus, keeping their bacteria-laden phlegm to themselves and their handkerchief, was one of the ways of combating TB. People who had contracted TB were nursed in isolation hospitals to curb the spread of the disease. By the time I had grown up, the 'No Spitting' signs had all gone, but hawking up and spitting on the street is now back in fashion. I saw a documentary about the increase of TB in our cities, and some who had contracted it were interviewed. They felt (and were encouraged in this direction by the questioning of the journalists) furious with the hospitals in whose wards they had contracted the illness. They were nursed in isolation not to protect others, but to protect themselves from opportunistic infections in their state of compromised immunity. Those who were most seriously ill, and could no longer be helped, were planning to go home. Is it just me? Or do you too want to say, 'Er... wait a minute... what about the risk of passing this dreadful illness on?'

In my adult years I have heard TB described as a poverty illness (and so it is). I have heard concerned, socially conscious Christians express the opinion that TB should be tackled by lifting people out of poverty – that is to say, throw money at it. But while we're waiting, could we not stop spitting on the street? And in some cases, might not a more responsible handling of the money we do (personally) have make a useful contribution towards increasing our health and well-being?

Responsibility is badly out of fashion: but nonetheless it is true that the ability to accept responsibility for our lives and conduct, for our families and property, and for our duty to act as good neighbours, will take our path into the road of blessing.

Irresponsible behaviour is a curse upon society. It disables and impoverishes, it leaves a trail of cynicism, sickness, misery and death.

For the Christian, Jesus has to be the ultimate role model for acceptance of responsibility. We gaze upon Jesus crucified, who saw what was required and was willing to assume responsibility for what he could do, that we could not do for ourselves. It enlarges forever the meaning of 'the buck stops here', and makes clear to us the connection between the willingness to accept responsibility and the way of blessing.

In the everyday rhythms of our ordinary lives, we will experience blessing as we establish norms of accepting responsibility and teaching those over whom we have influence to do the same.

My children, growing up together so close in age, were brought up to behave responsibly – the older children were especially expected to look out for their younger sisters. Our first family home had a large garden at the back of the house, and a smaller garden at the front. The front garden was an excellent place to play, because the living room opened directly onto it so that, as the door stood open in the summer the garden became an extension of the room. When my second child, Grace, was a toddler, as soon as she had finished her breakfast she liked to go out into the front garden. The first thing she did, this little tot with her curly hair, was to rush to the garden gate and close it so that she would not be in danger of wandering into the road. As a smaller, crawling baby, she must have seen me do this with her older sister, explaining that we must close the gate to keep the baby safely inside – and the importance of it impressed itself on Grace's mind.

In those days life seemed more relaxed. Seatbelts in cars existed but were not often worn, and our children used to sit in a row on the back seat of the car, behaving sensibly but not strapped in. The cars we owned in those days were a series of old bangers, erratic in performance. On one occasion as we drove along, one of the rear passenger doors swung open as we turned a corner. Grace, then two years old, was sitting adjacent to the door. As quick as a thought Rosie, her older sister, then just four, leaned across, grabbed the door and slammed it shut. All of us sometimes fail in our responsibilities. As parents, we should have ensured the door was shut tight: but sometimes we make mistakes. If *everyone* in the group has taken on board, as Rosie did, the need to look out for each other and accept responsibility, a fallback position is provided and calamity can often be averted.

Imagine a world in which everyone accepted responsibility: to be faithful to their marriage partners; to respect the property of others; to act for the well-being of creation and the natural environment; to educate themselves; to be gentle and considerate and forbearing with their children; to pay their bills; to tend their gardens for the delight of their neighbourhood; to dispose of their garbage responsibly; to repair, re-use, recycle; to curb their CO_2 emissions; to be cheerful, courteous, punctual, tidy, clean and kind.

Wouldn't that be a wonderful world? And yet, none of those things asks very much of us. Nobody has to be clever, or rich or exceptionally gifted to undertake such a programme. All it requires is the willingness to accept responsibility. Then we walk in the way of blessing. 'For God did not give us a spirit of timidity, but a spirit of power, of love and of self-discipline' (2 Timothy 1:7).

The acted prophecy of our lives

My whole life I will be grateful that I knew Martin Baddeley. He was the Principal of the Ordination Course where I trained for ministry, and the example of his humility, gentleness, patience and kindness was a Christian education in itself.

Like all good teachers, alongside and running through his lessons he wove in certain motifs, oft-repeated until his students could not help but memorize them, having heard them so often. One of Martin Baddeley's motifs was a question he taught us to ask. As we studied the Bible, as we prepared a sermon, as we made a decision, as we pastored a congregation – he taught us to ask, *What kind of God?* What kind of God is this affirming? What kind of God is this proclaiming? What kind of God will observers understand us to believe in?

The word of the Law and the Prophets in the lives of the people

The people of God in the Old Testament were shaped by story, liturgy, Law and prophecy.

> Tell it to your children, and let your children tell it to their children, and their children to the next generation.
>
> *Joel 1:3*

> Hear, O Israel: The Lord our God, the Lord is one. Love the Lord your God with all your heart and with all your soul and with all your strength. These commandments that I give you today are to be upon your hearts. Impress them on your children. Talk about them when you sit at home and when you walk along the road, when you lie

down and when you get up. Tie them as symbols on your
hands and bind them on your foreheads. Write them on
the door-frames of your houses and on your gates.

Deuteronomy 6:4–9

The story of the people of God and their covenant relationship
with the Almighty, of how he had saved and loved and watched
over and rescued and corrected them, was to be repeated and
remembered until it was part of their hearts and souls.

The Songs of Ascents, in the book of Psalms, were to
be sung antiphonally, calling and responding as the people of
God made their way in procession up to the sacred Temple on
Mount Zion.

The Law of Moses was to be the framework that shaped
their lives: like a growing tree carefully espaliered into the form
the gardener desires, or a bowl shaped on the turning wheel
according to the potter's conception, or wool knitted into a
pattern – the Law of Moses was their making; as it fashioned
their lives they became the people of God's promise.

And as they told the story, sang the liturgy, lived the
Law, the prophets provided an ongoing critique, a *leitmotif,*
a continual corrective shepherding them back into the way
of blessing. You can read any of the prophets you like, but
basically they are all saying the same two things:

1. You must offer true worship to the living God, orientating
    your life around him.
2. You must remember the poor and the afflicted, the
    stranger, the orphan, the widow, in mercy lifting them up
    so they too have a chance at happiness.

Wherever the prophets denounce and lambast the people, it is
always for the same two things:

1. Apostasy; turning aside from true worship of the living God to run after idols and offer fealty to worthless and inferior objects of devotion – be they beings or things.
2. Trampling on the poor, being ruthless and greedy and grabbing everything for self, cheating and exploiting people – most especially the poor and defenceless.

And in every case, the prophets emphasized the faithfulness of God. Sometimes they delivered their message in words and discourse; sometimes they acted out what they wanted to communicate, or placed images full of meaning before the people:

> The word of the Lord came to me again: 'What do you see?'
>
> 'I see a boiling pot, tilting away from the north,' I answered.
>
> The Lord said to me, 'From the north disaster will be poured out on all who live in the land.'
>
> *Jeremiah 1:13–14*

> Elisha said, 'Get a bow and some arrows,' and he [King Jehoash] did so. 'Take the bow in your hands,' he said to the king of Israel. When he had taken it, Elisha put his hands on the king's hands.
>
> 'Open the east window,' he said, and he opened it. 'Shoot!' Elisha said, and he shot. 'The Lord's arrow of victory, the arrow of victory over Aram!' Elisha declared. 'You will completely destroy the Arameans at Aphek.'
>
> *2 Kings 13:15–17*

These pregnant images, or acted prophecies, spoke more vividly than words alone, and communicated holistically the will of God for a specific situation – the feel of it, the tenor of it.

The Old Testament themes of justice and reconciliation fulfilled in Christ's life

As we move forward into the New Testament, we are led into a development of our understanding. The Old Testament is not wiped away and negated: that would be as if we built a foundation, then got rid of it because we had moved on to building walls now instead. The Law and the Prophets, the story and the worship, the covenant relationship of the people with God, all remain foundational to the Kingdom of Christ and the Gospel. In Christ the story, the worship, the Law, the Prophets and the people are fulfilled:

> For in Christ all the fulness of the Deity lives in bodily form… These are a shadow of the things that were to come; the reality, however, is found in Christ.
>
> *Colossians 2:9, 17*

> For in him dwelleth all the fulness of the Godhead bodily. And ye are complete in him…
>
> *Colossians 2:9–10a KJV*

> Do not think that I have come to abolish the Law or the Prophets; I have not come to abolish them but to fulfil them.
>
> *Matthew 5:17*

151

So also, when we were children, we were in slavery under the basic principles of the world. But when the time had fully come, God sent his Son, born of a woman, born under law, to redeem those under law, that we might receive the full rights of sons.

Galatians 4:3–5

From the fulness of his grace we have all received one blessing after another. For the law was given through Moses; grace and truth came through Jesus Christ.

John 1:16–17

The letter to the Colossians describes Jesus as gathering up all things into himself:

For God was pleased to have all his fulness dwell in him, and through him to reconcile to himself all things, whether things on earth or things in heaven, by making peace through his blood, shed on the cross.

Colossians 1:19–20

This created an inherent, existential, ontological unity, all people and everything in creation held together in Jesus Christ through his death on the cross.

In the days of the Old Testament, the power of God was expressed through the particular ministry of individuals – the patriarchs, the prophets and the priests. They were called into God's presence in a special and intimate way, they experienced God immediately, and then relayed what they had seen and heard in his presence to the people.

Then when Jesus the Messiah came into the world, everything was seen by comparison to have been partial: he completed it, he fulfilled it, he finished it. As he died on the cross, he cried out: 'It is finished!' Everything was joined, now. The way things are had a heart, and the heart was the cross of Jesus: it became the centre of living reality, the crossing place, the point of connection uniting every living thing. But even that was not the end of it.

The gospel writers show the way for us to lead prophetic lives

The gospels were written for a particular purpose. They are not biographies, or journals, or propaganda. They are not written to convince or convert (though they do).

The gospels were written for the church, for the first followers of Jesus after the Ascension had taken place. They were written to answer the question, 'Now what?' Because Jesus had gone from their sight. What did it mean, to say he had risen? In what sense could it be said, he is with us?

Christ's life prophesies of God's inclusive and redemptive love in Luke's gospel

In the gospel of Luke, Christ is the healer of humankind, the physician of our souls; full of compassion, restoring and lifting up the strayed and the forgotten.

Luke's gospel, taken together as it should be with the book of Acts, describes the unfolding, the exploding, of the Gospel. In his gospel, it starts as a revolutionary seed; the hope of all people. We see Mary the mother of Jesus with her defiant song of protest that echoes the prophets and is re-echoed by Jesus as he begins his public ministry in Luke 4. We see an unwed mother, an older formerly barren woman, a babe *in utero,* all filled with and responding to the Holy Spirit. We see angels visiting *shepherds*: the day of the marginalized has come! Luke writes of the lost gathered up and found. When he tells the story of the ninety-nine sheep left on the hillside while the shepherd goes off seeking the stray, unlike Matthew (18:12–13) who writes, 'and *if* he finds it…', Luke (15:4–7) writes, 'and *when* he finds it…'

He writes of Zacchaeus (Luke 19:9–10): 'Today salvation has come to this house, because this man, too, is a son of Abraham. For the Son of Man came to seek and to save what was lost.'

'This man, too, is a son of Abraham.' Luke's gospel begins and ends in Jerusalem. Focuses upon Jerusalem. In the temptation narrative, when Jesus is driven into the wilderness by the Spirit at the start of his ministry, Matthew (4:8) gives us the mountain as the climax of the temptations, whereas Luke (4:9) gives us the temple. Luke's gospel is based at Jerusalem, the centre of the faith, the home of the temple of the children of Abraham.

But Part Two, the book of Acts, shows what happens when the seed begins to grow. It is unstoppable. The seed of the Gospel that begins at Jerusalem, the heart of the world of faith, grows and spreads – the book of Acts concludes in Rome, the heart of the secular world. Luke is telling us that the Gospel is for every part of life and for all people: that there are no divisions now between sacred and secular, between who's in and who's out – in Christ the whole world can come home. And the Spirit of Christ, because of the Ascension and Pentecost, is poured out upon all people. No more is the experience of the Spirit contained within the particular ministry of special individuals – patriarchs, prophets and priests: it is open and available to the whole people of God; and with the privilege goes the responsibility.

Christ's life speaks of God's luminous majesty in John's gospel

In the gospel of John, Jesus is a cosmic and priestly figure. The cross in this gospel is described in terms of an hour of glory: a climactic moment in which light blazes out, overflows and floods the whole cosmos. Jesus is seen as a light moving through a dark world, bringing illumination:

> In him was life, and that life was the light of men. The light shines in the darkness, but the darkness has not understood it… The true light that gives light to every man was coming into the world… We have seen his glory, the glory of the One and Only, who came from the Father, full of grace and truth.

> *John 1:4–5, 9, 14*

In his stories of the resurrection, John draws out of us an understanding of the way the light that came to us in Jesus has now illuminated the whole people of God, the whole body of Christ.

> Early on the first day of the week, while it was still dark, Mary Magdalene went to the tomb and saw that the stone had been removed from the entrance. So she came running to Simon Peter and the other disciple, the one Jesus loved, and said, 'They have taken the Lord out of the tomb, and we don't know where they have put him!'
>
> So Peter and the other disciple started for the tomb. Both were running, but the other disciple outran Peter

and reached the tomb first. He bent over and *looked in
at* the strips of linen lying there but did not go in. Then
Simon Peter, who was behind him, arrived and went into
the tomb. He *saw* the strips of linen lying there, as well
as the burial cloth that had been around Jesus' head. The
cloth was folded up by itself, separate from the linen.
Finally the other disciple, who had reached the tomb first,
also went inside. He *saw* and believed.

John 20:1–8 (italics mine)

'Saw', or 'looked at' – this occurs three times in this passage.
The beloved disciple *saw* the strips of linen; Peter *saw* the strips
of linen; finally the beloved disciple went right in – he *saw*
and he believed. In the Greek, this 'seeing' uses three different
verbs delineating a progression: to glimpse, to examine, to
understand. This progression is a model for us as disciples. The
Light is at first outside us, beyond us; then we open ourselves
to it, ponder it and meditate upon it; then it enlightens us,
illuminates us, so that we ourselves become people of the
Light, shining in a dark world.

In his story of doubting Thomas (John 20:19–29), John
sketches out for us the rhythm of the worshipping church, the
eucharistic gathering on the first day of the week where, if we
come, we will have the chance to experience for ourselves the
presence of the risen Lord. In similar wise Luke (24:13–35)
draws a picture for us of disciples who encounter Christ in the
stranger, as they open the scriptures and share in the breaking
of the bread, the hospitality of the Lord's table.

Luke and John are drawing us on to see how Christ
breaks open and at the same time fulfils all the old moulds
and frameworks. The same Spirit that was in Jesus is now in

the gathered community of the people of God: the Light that came into the world is still potent to enlighten our hearts and minds.

Matthew and Mark engage upon the same task.

Christ's life models the faithful Israel in Matthew's gospel

Where Luke presents Jesus as offering healing to broken humanity, and John shows him as the light come to illuminate a dark world, Matthew portrays him as a teacher of righteousness, the fulfilment of Israel. Like Moses, in Matthew's gospel Christ takes refuge in Egypt and returns to his people from there. Matthew structures his gospel to portray Christ offering five blocks of teaching reminiscent of the books of Moses, the Pentateuch. In Matthew's gospel, mountains have particular significance, for in the Old Testament mountains are the place of God's special self-revelation and imparting of the Law. So in Matthew, Luke's Sermon on the Plain is a Sermon on the Mount.

In Matthew's temptation narrative, Mark's original and starkly simple outline of a place of wild beasts and angels is expanded to echo the journey of Israel through the wilderness (for the Old Testament quotations Jesus uses to refute the Devil draw upon specific incidents in the ancient history of Israel, when the people tempted God and let him down), culminating in the temptation on the mountain-top, always the place of God's meeting with Moses. Matthew is showing us Christ as the faithfulness that Israel could not muster, the consummation of the covenant relationship with God. He completes and brings home what was begun so long ago. And as we have seen earlier, Matthew also addresses the Gentile component of his congregation, showing that they too are made complete in Christ.

Christ's life reveals that God is with us in Mark's gospel

Mark's gospel, source for much of the material used by the other evangelists, has to be one of the most elegantly concise documents ever written. Terse and spare in his style, Mark goes to the heart of the matter and portrays Jesus simply as the Son of God.

Mark has a particular literary technique that some people refer to as 'sandwiches'! He likes to start a story (first slice of bread), interrupt it with a related story (filling) and then return to finish off the first story (second slice of bread). An example of this technique is the story (Mark 5:21–43) of the healing of Jairus' daughter, a twelve-year-old girl (so presumably around the menarche), interrupted by the story of the healing of the woman who had been troubled by bleeding (so probably related to menopause) for twelve years.

But this literary technique is also applied to the whole structure of Mark's gospel: its very structure is of itself a teaching tool. Mark's gospel begins with the briefest of prologues: 'The beginning of the gospel about Jesus Christ the Son of God.' This is his central theme.

The next thing that happens is the baptism of Jesus, in which the heavens are torn open and the voice of God is heard, saying, 'You are my Son, whom I love; with you I am well pleased' (Mark 1:11). Then Jesus retreats into the wilderness, then his ministry begins in earnest.

The first words we hear Jesus say in Mark's gospel (Mark 1:15) are: 'The time has come... The kingdom of God is near.

Repent and believe the good news!'

We should pay special attention to this, because in the case of each gospel, the first words Jesus speaks are indicative of the theme central to the gospel. In Matthew, Jesus' first words are (to John the Baptist): 'Let it be so now; it is proper for us to do this to fulfil all righteousness' (3:15) – and the fulfilment of all righteousness is exactly what Matthew shows us Jesus doing. In John, who shows us Jesus as the Light by which our inner being can be illuminated, the first words of Jesus are (John 1:38–39, my paraphrase): 'What are you looking for?… Come, and you will see.' Luke, who goes to such lengths to include the marginalized, the small and peripheral people, and show us that they too can be filled with the Holy Spirit, has Jesus speak first as a child (Luke 2:49): 'Why were you searching for me?… Didn't you know I had to be in my Father's house?' (Remember Luke's focus on Jerusalem and the temple.)

But Mark, sometimes known as an 'action gospel', cracks right on with things: 'The time has come… The kingdom of God is near. Repent and believe the good news!' The Son of God has come to realize his Kingdom. Talk about 'hit the ground running'!

Mark next unfolds before us the ministry of Jesus in signs and wonders, healing the sick, exorcising demons and demonstrating power over the elements. Wherever he goes, people are asking in wonder, 'Who is this?'

Who is this, who can forgive sins? Who is this, who can heal the sick? Who is this, who can cast out demons? Who is this, who teaches with such authority? Who is this, that even the wind and waves obey him? The only ones who recognize and identify him are the evil spirits (because they are supernatural entities) and the reader (who has had the benefit of the prologue).

Several chapters are given over to describing the ministry of Jesus in miracles, teaching and parables, and conveying the sense of immense challenge implicit in who he was and what he did. That's the first slice of bread, in this daddy-burger of a literary sandwich.

Then, in chapter 8, we move on to the central section (the 'filling'). This section opens with the first of two healings of the blind (Mark 8:22–25), that of the blind man at Bethsaida. The section will close with a second healing.

In this first of the two healings, not mentioned by the other evangelists, who are less comfortable than Mark with portraying Jesus as not enjoying instant success, Jesus has to make two attempts at healing the man before his sight is clear. The first time, Jesus asks him if he can see, and he says yes, but not clearly: then Jesus applies further ministry, and the man can see properly. In the gospels sight is used as a metaphor for insight.

The next thing that happens is Peter's famous confession of faith. 'Who do people say I am?' Jesus asks his disciples (Mark 8:27): and we know that the chapters so far have been ringing with the question, 'Who is this?' Like eager children in class, we want to shoot up our hands – 'Ooh! Ask me! I know!' – because we have read the prologue, and we know that this is the Son of God.

Jesus then brings the question home: 'But what about you?… Who do you say I am?' And Peter responds: 'You are the Christ' (Mark 8:29).

Mark leads us towards an understanding of how we must live this radical truth

Now we come to the heart of things. The gospel of Mark is written to change our understanding of what it means to be the Messiah. At the time Jesus came, the Jews were looking for a great leader to restore their fallen fortunes, to usher in a new golden age like that of King David, to overthrow the oppressor. In the Messiah, they were expecting a victorious king. Now comes the task of trying to communicate that the power of God works through weakness: that the Messiah will bring about salvation not by hammering the enemy into a pulp but by laying down his own life; what Jesus has to get across is virtually incomprehensible. The Messiah is supposed to be not merely victorious but totally invincible. He has to turn their whole understanding around.

So now Jesus begins to teach that he must suffer, and be rejected, and put to death: and Peter, believing him to be the Messiah with all that implies, as well as loving him with his whole heart, rebukes him for saying it. Jesus responds with stern words (Mark 8:33): 'Get behind me, Satan!... You do not have in mind the things of God, but the things of men.' And Jesus then unfolds before them urgently and plainly the necessity of the cross, as much for those who follow as for their Lord.

Peter, we realize, was the blind man who saw but not properly; who had been enlightened, but needed further enlightenment before he would really see. Jesus hammers home that his ministry, his Kingdom, his power is *spiritual*, not political: 'What good is it for a man to gain the whole world, yet forfeit his soul? Or what can a man give in

161

exchange for his soul?' (Mark 8:36–37).

We come now to the pinnacle of Mark's gospel – literally; it happens on a mountain. Christ is transfigured. His disciples are dazzled as he appears before them gloriously robed in white, flanked by Moses (the Law) and Elijah (the Prophets). Underlining and emphasizing all that he has taught them in re-defining the role of Messiah as suffering servant, a voice comes from heaven: 'This is my Son, whom I love. *Listen* to him!' (Mark 9:7).

They come down from the mountain, and Jesus has occasion to speak to them about prayer, humility, inclusiveness, purity, integrity; all crucial aspects of his redefined Kingdom. He teaches them further about the necessity of suffering, his teaching culminating in the summary (Mark 10:44–45): 'whoever wants to be first must be slave of all. For even the Son of Man did not come to be served, but to serve, and to give his life as a ransom for many.'

Then the section closes with a second healing of a blind man (Bartimaeus, in chapter 10). Bartimaeus addresses him (at the top of his voice, and will not be dissuaded) as 'Son of David', which is what the Messiah had to be. Jesus asks him what he wants, and he answers: 'Rabbi, I want to *see*' (verse 51) – and sight, we remember, is also a metaphor for insight. Jesus heals him, this time the healing going through with no hitches, and Bartimaeus 'followed Jesus in the way' (verse 52, my paraphrase): which is to say, he became a believer.

So, we have a prologue, a voice from heaven, an opening 'Who is this?' section; then a central section redefining the role of the Messiah in terms of suffering servanthood, bracketed within two healings of sight that also act as a metaphor for the ability of the disciples (all of us, but represented by Peter) to really see what is meant: the zenith of that central section being the Mount of Transfiguration, with the second voice from heaven.

After that, we are straight into the entry into Jerusalem: Mark's gospel has been called a passion narrative with an introduction – its focus is the cross, and this last third of the text is given over to that story.

There is further teaching driving home the lesson, his anointing at Bethany, his betrayal, his trial, his crucifixion.

> Those who passed by hurled insults at him, shaking their heads and saying, 'So! You who are going to destroy the temple and build it in three days, come down from the cross and save yourself!'
>
> In the same way the chief priests and the teachers of the law mocked him among themselves. 'He saved others,' they said, 'but he can't save himself! Let this Christ, this King of Israel, come down now from the cross, that we may see and believe.'
>
> *Mark 15:29–32*

We who have been privileged to travel this far with Mark have grasped by now what it really means to 'see and believe', and this dreadful irony is not lost upon us.

Then comes the most moving moment (for me) of Mark's gospel:

> The curtain of the temple was torn in two from top to bottom. And when the centurion, who stood there in front of Jesus, heard his cry and saw how he died, he said, 'Surely this man was the Son of God!'
>
> *Mark 15:38–39*

For the third time, in the rending of the temple curtain, heaven is torn open. The curtain is torn from top to bottom this time: no going back – it is accomplished.

For the third time comes a voice saying that this is the Son of God: but this time it is not a voice from heaven, but Earth's reply; the centurion, not a disciple, not even a Jew. A pagan, an unnamed outsider: the Gospel has gone out into all the world.

The torch is passed into our hands, for we are to be the body of Christ now

Just as Luke shows us the seed of the Gospel spreading from Jerusalem to Rome; just as John shows us the Light that came into the world, flooding the heart of every believer; just as Matthew shows us the best aspirations of Jew and Gentile alike fulfilled in Jesus – so Mark comes to rest on his keynote: truly, this man (the suffering servant) was the Son of God.

Hallelujah! *Woohoo!!* Amen!

So it is that the gospel writers enable us to see that the power and presence of God that we saw in awe and majesty in the Old Testament, was there full throttle in the humility of Jesus: and that as we walk in his way in the company of believers, that power is also made present in us. We are no longer dependent on the mediation of prophets and priests; at Pentecost, his Spirit is poured out upon all flesh:

> … You are a chosen people, a royal priesthood, a holy
> nation, a people belonging to God, that you may declare
> the praises of him who called you out of darkness into his
> wonderful light.
>
> *1 Peter 2:9*

What this means is that the *whole of our lives* now becomes an acted prophecy: because the way of blessing, being Christian, following Jesus, living in the Spirit, is more than what we do – it's what we are.

As we take up the torch of the holy Gospel to live it and breathe it in every moment so that people can see its glory and be offered the chance to reach out and take hold of it for themselves, we are dealing with a heady concept that must be earthed into ordinary everyday reality.

We take our cue first of all from the pictures the four gospel writers show us: that Jesus is Lord, that he is our fulfilment, that he heals us, that he had a humble, servant heart, that he loves to the uttermost, and that his great glory is rooted in his self-giving regardless of cost. If our lives are to become acted prophecies about the lordship of Jesus, demonstrating that the only power is God whose love transforms and redeems all creation through Jesus' death on the cross, that's a costly mission we've taken on! And we are only ordinary people. How might we go about it?

I have a friend who taught herself dressmaking. She said at first she found the whole idea too daunting to contemplate. She looked at the sewing machine and the fabric in the shop and the end product she was supposed to be putting together, and she knew in her heart: 'I can't do that'. But when she opened up the instructions that came with the pattern, she asked herself: 'Well, can I manage Step 1?' And she found the answer came back, 'Yes. I can.' So she did Step 1.

Once she'd completed Step 1, she could see what was meant in the instructions for Step 2. When Step 2 had been accomplished, the directions for Step 3 began to make sense: until by and by she held a dress in her hands.

When we launch into the re-conceptualising of our lives as acted prophecies of the Lord's power and glory, naturally the project seems a little intimidating. So we break it into steps, and work on them one at a time. It's not on the to-do list for a quiet weekend, it's our magnum opus, the great work of a lifetime.

To do it successfully we have to give it space. We shall be aiming to reach the place where our personal holiness shines like a light to lead people to Jesus: our words, our actions, our attitudes, how we run our household, how we dress, what we read or watch on TV, our demeanour, our purchases, our politics – the minutiae of our lives. Everything about us will be drawn into the one-focus purpose of living our lives as an acted prophecy of the kind of God we know and love and serve. Such an endeavour will eventually grow to a stature where it will be sturdy enough to withstand opposition and pressure; but especially at first, it will need lots of space around it. We are more likely to get our decisions right if we give ourselves time to think carefully and to pray; and that will mean learning to be disciplined about our schedules, keeping things simple so we aren't always working from unexamined thinking we've been taught and taken for granted, trying to tackle everything on the run.

With each step we undertake, we follow a simple procedure.

First we pick out what aspect of our discipleship we would like to work on – perhaps, say, we would like to improve on gracious and gentle speech, building others up with kind and encouraging words.

Then, having established a clear discipleship goal, next we merge that goal with our imagination: we read articles and books and sermons and scriptures about kind and loving speech and the power of encouragement, we seek out the company of friends who shine in this area, we read novels that pick up the theme, we cry out to God in our prayer time to bring about this aspect of discipleship in our personal witness, we get ourselves into the place where we have grasped it imaginatively, so that we have the feel and the flavour of it internalised, not just viewed from afar, sighing, 'I wish!'

Having chosen a specific goal and merged with it imaginatively, next we lock it firmly in place. How might we do that? We safeguard ourselves with reminders: ask a friend or prayer partners to support us in achieving our goal by gentle admonishment and jogging our memory. Maybe we wear a ring or item of clothing – or the old-fashioned trick of making a knot in our handkerchiefs – to help recall to mind that we said we would do this. It might help to set a time goal, perhaps 'I will focus primarily on this for forty days' (the time they say it takes to establish a new habit).

Next, having chosen it, merged with it imaginatively and locked it in place, we begin to act upon it: practice it, actually consciously do it.

Then, finally – and this is the difficult part – we persevere with it, and do not ever give up.

So, step by step we draw our ordinary daily lives into an alignment wth the life of Christ, building confidently on the foundations he has laid for us, knowing that we don't have to wait until we get it perfect because every kind word, every loving action, every movement of forgiveness is already an acted prophecy revealing the kind of God we serve.

And we follow the pattern of the prophets of old, who first were called into the presence of God's holiness and then were sent out to reveal his truth. In similar wise we start by coming quietly to God in private prayer, listening for the prompting of his transforming word speaking in the silence of our hearts, and then we set out on the path of daily life to make known, by all we choose and do and are, what God is like.

So in the final analysis, the road of blessing comes down to this: stepping into the glorious light of the Son of God; understanding who he was and what he came here to do; and allowing ourselves to be saturated by his Spirit, so that whatever happens to us passes through the alchemy of his grace, his love, his power.

'Walking in the Way', as Mark's gospel puts it, following in the road of blessing, is a matter of living the Scripture:

> ...I no longer live, but Christ lives in me. The life I live in the body, I live by faith in the Son of God, who loved me and gave himself for me.
>
> *Galatians 2:20*

We find the words of the sermon on the mount come true:

> Focus on the Kingdom of God in your lives and make it your first priority, and you will find that your physical circumstances and condition simply fall into place.
>
> *Matthew 6:33 (my paraphrase)*

It would be unrealistic to pretend this way is not costly: 'You are not your own; you were bought at a price' (1 Corinthians 6:19–20); all I have and am belongs to Christ if I have opened my heart to him and invited him in to be my Lord – and he may at any time require me to return or lay down or step back from what I had come to regard as my own affair, my own possessions, my own business. But those who choose to walk in this way because they love him, find the rewards worthwhile: the sweetness of his presence, which is joy and peace indescribable; the harmony and fulfilment discovered in moving with the flow of God's creative power instead of engaging in the sterile struggle against it.

For me, what is most exciting of all is the growing sense of being part of something really, really big. I haven't got very far along the road of blessing, but the meaning and the miracles, the 'coincidences' and the prayers answered, the loving-kindness of God's provision, the peace and contentment – they amaze me. I look at the stars flung across the night sky, at the colours of the sunrise and the swell of the sea, and I think: 'I am part of that – I have my place in the pattern into which all this is woven.'

And somewhere, if I listen carefully, I think I hear a divine whisper, saying, 'Yeah, baby – and you ain't seen nothing yet!'

Questions and Answers

The manuscript of *The Road of Blessing* was sent out to a number of honest and intelligent readers in its final stages before publication, with the request that they come back to me with the questions that arose in their minds as they read it. This they did. I wish I had space to answer all their questions here, for they were so probing and far-reaching; they did a brilliant job, my band of readers! One of them threw in a bonus too, in teaching me for the first time in my life the correct use of the semi-colon.

Here follows as great a selection as space allows of the questions they asked me, in their own words.

What's a 'Prosperity Gospel' book, and how is it different from *The Road of Blessing*?

Prosperity Gospel teaching encourages people to aspire to and rejoice in wealth and abundance, and can cite many texts from the Bible in support of this aspiration. I believe that the road of blessing starts with and stays with simplicity. It is lowly and frugal, it aspires to be the lowest and the least, peaceful and unnoticed, humble and of no account. No bling. No private jet. No mansion. No offshore accounts to avoid tax on my massive bank account. Simply enough and the grace to know when we have enough: 'give us this day our daily bread'.

I believe that where money gathers, so do jealousy and relational imbalances. In the words of Toinette Lippe, 'Problems arise where things accumulate.' The road of blessing avoids accumulation. It stays close to simplicity. It is a hedgerow path, a sheeptrack, it walks the wild and quiet ways, asking for little, content to serve, loving prayer and peace.

Though we are called to be responsible for our own spiritual paths, we get help from things like this book. But how can we help mentally disabled people find the path of blessing?

We can't really help someone else; each of us has to do it for ourselves. Each of us is able and disabled – the politically correct phrase 'differently abled' is clunky but actually very accurate. Anyone who spends time around them knows that people with learning disabilities are more likely to show us the road of blessing than the other way round. I think they probably came here as teachers, helping to put us in touch with compassion, vulnerability, the power of honest human relationship, and a different way of looking at the world.

If we are travelling through life with a differently abled friend ('learning disabled' is the current politically correct term in the UK, but I have found it to be something of a misnomer, as many of those to whom it is applied learn some things very fast indeed) there is no difference between how we show them the road of blessing and how we show anyone else. There is only one way – do it yourself. The response is almost always the same at first. Those who are observing you have a thousand reasons why it wouldn't work for them, why it's only luck, why their circumstances and personality mean it would never work for them. They have to try it for a while; and then they see. Finding the way of blessing in the first place can happen through rational analytical thinking, but it is more likely to be intuitional, accidental, or through sheer desperation – which is perhaps why learning disabled people find their way to it often with such grace and ease.

On those occasions when life has given me responsibility for someone with special needs, I have taught them the road of blessing in the same way I teach others; by living it and by letting its principles shape my expectations and requirements in my relationships. If one of my children had been disabled, I should have brought her or him up in the road of blessing, as I did my own children. It is a disciplined way as well as kind.

If you're having a bad day, or even a bad moment, what do you find helpful for getting you back in the right way or mindset for the road of blessing?

When that happens, I try to get by myself, slow down, and give myself a treat. If I am writing, I take a break and read a book or watch a film – my very favourite film is Philip Groening's *Into Great Silence* which, if I were rewriting the Bible, I would slip into the 23rd Psalm along with the green pastures and still waters as one of the means of restoring a weary soul.

A bad day for me is synonymous with a high-pressure day: too many people, too much to achieve and attend to, a crowded schedule. Its badness consists in my getting steamed up and stressed, talking too much, and letting off steam like an over-heated pressure cooker. I give myself space or, if that cannot be done, I am trying the new (to me) and amazingly successful experiment of explaining that I cannot manage and asking for help.

There are three phrases that are keys to the road of blessing: 'Thank you', 'I love you', and 'I'm sorry'. Everything we say, think or do should be able loosely to be categorized under one of those headings. Everything else trips us up and wastes our time.

If miracles flower by following along the road of blessing and always being truthful, how come sometimes you hear of people performing miracles who later turned out to be bad in some way – deceitful or abusive?

Ooh, this is a conundrum, isn't it! I have known some people like this. I notice that the truth usually catches up with them in the end, and I think in the grand scheme of things this will be true in every case: 'The truth will find you out' is the old proverb, and it will indeed – not to punish you, but to set you free. Anyone who has woven a web of lies is trapped inside them, and God in compassion will not leave them there, He will let them out.

Meanwhile until that moment of truth comes, what a puzzle this is! Judas was a good example. He was the treasurer for the band of disciples following Jesus, and used to help himself to the money, which apparently they all knew. Yet he was still in the group that was sent out to heal and exorcise.

I guess that all of us fall short and have our character weaknesses. We are all sinful. That's why we are all subjected to sickness and death. That's why Jesus was unique, in all ways as we are except without sin. So those people who do miracles despite their imperfections probably differ from the rest of us in that at least they believe without hesitation in the miracles. Those of us who feel shaky on the belief front need to rest in the truth – our belief is weak, so we are relying on steeping our lives in truth to make the miracles come.

What did you mean, when you said about 'feet being our self-understanding'?

There is something funny about feet. Reflexologists can map your whole body on your feet and treat the different parts of the body through the feet. I like the idea of the underneath of your feet being a sole (soul). When Moses came to the burning bush, God said 'Take off your shoes for you are on holy ground'. I never understand why we take no notice of that bit of the Bible; I take my shoes off when I go into church. I believe it is important to spend as much time in bare feet as is practical. It keeps me in contact and tuned in. And our self-understanding? Well, they are – aren't they? When we are standing, our feet are underneath us: self-under-standing; see? It is simple fact and it is also a metaphor for something bigger. Everything is held in context of the meta-narrative, and the meta-narrative is spiritual.

When you observe that people who are dear to you are not on the road of blessing, what do you do? Do you talk to them openly about it? Pray? If so, how do you pray for loved ones who do not choose to put their feet on the road of blessing?

There is not much you can do for people in terms of telling them. I have written this book to discharge my responsibility in this regard; when they are ready to know, they will come across the book. I have found that all the people who live with me gradually tune into this path and come to understand it, but when they go away and fall under other influences, they gradually forget. They know really though, they are just dozing; they have the capacity to wake up. Well, we all do. Really all you can do is show people; telling them tends to antagonize. They come up with numerous reasons why you must be wrong, why it is all luck and circumstance – and there is nothing to be gained by arguing. Either they see it or they don't. And if they try it they will see it.

When you went through your divorce and lost your home and income, were you aware that you were or were not (then) on the road of blessing? Does this road seem more difficult to walk when things are (have been) falling apart around you?

There have been a number of times now when things seemed to be falling to pieces around me. I have been divorced after a marriage of twenty-four years, then I married my second husband, Bernard, who died fifteen months into our marriage. I married again a year later, and my new marriage involved a complete uprooting from my family. Amidst the rubble of these various situations I kept walking and I kept my eyes firmly fixed where I wanted to be. What broke my heart in the ending of my first marriage was the smashing of my home and family. What I had longed for was the time when my children would be adult and bring into the family home all their wisdom and life experience, their partners and children, their thoughts and insights and dreams; and it was all gone, all broken before we got there. I wanted it back.

Now, ten years later, I have a large house and those members of my family who are single live in community there with me and my husband. The house is big enough for family gatherings. We have a Bechstein piano so we can sing carols at Christmas and hymns at our fellowship nights. We have a beautiful garden where my grandson can play and the animals and birds can come, and we have planted lots of trees. In the meantime, as I kept walking, friends bringing love and support came from nowhere, money materialized, love came to me. I had nothing. I took no vengeance. When we separated, I sent my first husband on his way freely, with no strings, no settlement giving me rights to part of his old age pension. His children did not even in their thoughts reproach him. I blessed him on his way, feeling that the new love he had found should have its chance – and he is very happy with his new wife, they are right for each other, they bring each other joy. There is no need to be vengeful when somebody hurts you; life is just, it will rebalance. There is no need to make a grab for their money; the world is full of money, if you walk in the right way what you need will come to you in abundance. This is what Jesus said: *Seek first the kingdom of God and all these things will be added unto you.*

When my husband left, I was shattered, I was broken-hearted, I felt like a crater of ashes; but I knew the road of blessing, so I knew how to rebuild. It was not more difficult to walk the road then, it was totally essential. It was my only hope. The peculiar circumstances meant I had lost the only means of earning money I was trained for, so I went to the matron of a care home where I had been a chaplain, and asked her for a job. She had no jobs to offer as it is an excellent care home and so was well-provided with staff – people aspire to work there. D'you know what she did? She created me a job, made a space for me. She set my wages at the highest level for care assistants even though I had no training at all, because she said she knew the quality of what I could bring. The road of blessing is for good times and bad: if you follow it, you will never run out of hope. The adversity provides the stones for you to build the way and make it strong. If you follow the road of blessing your adversity will become your strength.

What are the (have been the) biggest stumbling blocks for you as you walk this road? What things/situations/ challenges do you have to be most careful of personally, to make sure you stay on this road?

I am by nature an anxious person, and with that comes a certain personal insecurity and desire to please others. In following the road of blessing my biggest stumbling block is that this anxiety, this sense of personal inadequacy, diminishes my capacity for generosity: I criticize others and I complain. How I am learning to overcome this is not by attacking the negative habits of complaining and criticizing, but by living a very gentle and spacious life so that my tendency to anxiety is not activated by more pressure than I can handle. I am learning not to take on too much, to let things go, and to give myself time and space. My second biggest stumbling block is that I talk too much. Silence builds the spirit. Spirit flows, and where there is silence it creates a pool; it doesn't dam the spirit, the flow goes on, but it creates a kind of glade with a pool, a place where spirit widens peacefully and others can approach and drink. I am learning about silence and gradually coaxing myself into speaking less and spending more time in solitude.

You share a home with several family members – are they all firmly committed to simplicity and the road of blessing? If you lived with someone who was not willing to embrace these ways, what would be your response?

Yes. The people I live with are wise. They are like spiritual masters. They are teachers of the road of blessing. Their wise teaching blows me away. I wish you could meet them and learn from them. They are amazing. Nobody listens to them, nobody notices them, they slip through the world like a quiet intriguing river of peace, unremarked and overlooked, holding the secrets of life. They are the Little Ones of God. They own very few possessions, they work in occupations that create beauty and kindness and do no harm, they practise generosity and simplicity and frugality and honesty, they speak little and love deeply. They live on microscopic incomes and by sharing and simplicity still accrue savings in the bank. The people I live with are beautiful and astonishing, and they encourage me every day. My husband, for example, the only one of us whose income even reaches let alone exceeds £10,000 a year, spends hardly anything on himself and gives away most of what he earns to support and help others.

What would be my response if I had to live with someone unwilling to embrace these ways? I would bless them, and move out.

Have you had to let any good friendships go because of the paths you've taken?

Yes, I have. And some not so good friendships. I have tried to remain at peace and in good fellowship with everyone in my life, because they are all there for a reason, and they are all part of God's love towards me. But sometimes it is important to set boundaries, especially when people with strong agendas want to annex my life or include me as a bit part in their chaotic dramas. Then I decline. It is never forever, and I bear nobody any ill will. God bless them. But I have to operate strong and clear boundaries with some people whom I might have expected to be more relaxed with. It is very important though that I continue to love them very much. Hatred and resentment create strong binding cords that hold the ones you hate and resent close to you in tight relationship. If there is someone you urgently need to move out of your life, you have to sincerely love them. It's the only way to get rid of them. Love brings freedom and love is God's agenda; he will keep bringing back to you the people and situations where you cannot love, in kindness to you, because you must learn to love or you cannot be made whole.

Since the road of blessing can be a road that even some Christians don't yet walk, have you had a difficult time finding other kindred souls on this path? Have you felt the need to fellowship often with people who live as you do?

I need very much the fellowship of other people who live this way. Very much. And they are not easy to find, not because they aren't there, but because they live quietly and unobtrusively. They are hard to see. They never interfere or push themselves forward. The kindred walk on quiet, hidden paths. They are like gold dust. I don't need to see them often – sometimes months or even years go by; but we are linked in, and their fellowship brings me so much encouragement.

Has there ever been a time or season in your Christian life when you believed deeply, but were not serene and peaceful? You seem like such a peaceful soul, yet I wonder if you've ever wailed in despair, wallowed in hopelessness? During the years of your divorce did anything like this characterize your life? Has the road of blessing greatly relieved any depression you've ever had?

I come from a family for whom psychiatric illness (principally anxiety and depression) is the norm. Walking the road of blessing allows me to understand myself and to live in peace and well-being without medication. I am not so constructed as to be able to participate very much in the world; I cannot

179

do a job in the normal sense, but it doesn't matter because I am on the road of blessing and I am held in the hand of God. I get angry and unhappy and bitter, I experience despair and grief and terror like any person; we all do. The important thing is living life in the light of something greater than myself; it gives my emotional weather perspective. I have a context; I am held in the hand of God.

Do you feel it's important to attend a church where others hold firmly to simplicity and the road of blessing as you know it?

Yes. Unfortunately I have come across such church communities only twice: the Poor Clare nuns, and the Bruderhof community (similar to Amish or Mennonites). I believe from what I have read that the Amish also hold firmly to simplicity. I feel called to marriage and called to faithfulness to the already existing relationships in my life – my friends, my family of origin, my husband and children. If I were a single, childless person I would join one of those church communities, because I believe that simplicity is the key to all spiritual development, and to live with others who also believe that is very strengthening. The household in which I live does practise that belief, and consequently, though we do all attend church in the normal sense, they are my real church community.

When you were in ministry to churches, did you preach the road of blessing often? If so, was it ever roundly rejected?

It informed all my preaching for about twenty years, during which time my own understanding of it developed and my confidence in it stood firm. I was well-received as a preacher and people enjoyed listening to me. They never rejected what

I had to say; they found me intriguing and amusing. But I did not form the impression that they were interested in applying the same principles to their lives. I am no longer an ordained minister in the church, so they no longer ask me to preach or teach; now, my life preaches. I am content with that, because George Fox, Gandhi, St Francis and my Lord Jesus all urged us to let our lives be the speaking of our message. When I preached in church, I think people did not really hear me; when they look at my life I do not think they see its message. It's something you have to try for yourself. And then you understand.

Have you ever found prayer difficult? Or a duty? If so, what happens to change it to a delight? What are some practical ways that you keep your gaze upon God all throughout the day?

How does the wave stay in the ocean? Where else is there to go? My life is held in God's hand. He keeps his gaze on me, and I feel it. I cannot tell if my prayer is chaotic and completely lacking in discipline or the unceasing heartbeat of my life. When I was a child I had a terror of losing my mother in a crowd when we were shopping. Losing sight of her in the grocer's store among the throng of people, I would look round wildly until I spotted the familiar tweed of her coat. I was frightened when we went on the underground trains in London that the doors would close before I had been able to follow her on, and I would be shut out, I would lose her. The same happens now with God. I get lost, and I look round wildly, and there he is. I am afraid of losing him, of being too slow to follow, and finding myself cut off, shut out. It has never happened so far. I guess there is always that risk, so I try to stay close to him: but I think really what's happening is that he is watching for me, and looking after me; he would come and look for me if I got lost, and search until he found me.

Do you ever have trouble loving people?

I am not by nature a very loving person. I am solitary, and I find human interaction difficult and puzzling. I often misjudge social situations and cause offence. I avoid human company, and usually regret it when I don't. I think there is something quite autistic in my personality. I detach very easily, and attach hardly at all. But I have a horror of hurting people, and I can both see and anticipate how they will feel. The thing that upsets me most in life is torture. I hate to see people humiliated or hurt. I tend to dislike and distrust very easily, and can be quick to criticize: but I don't want to wound people I dislike, just get away from them. So I have trouble staying close to people: I usually find myself desperately needing to be alone before they are done with spending time with me; but I delight in bringing people healing and comfort and peace, even if I strongly dislike them. I want them to be happy. I want them to be at ease in the world, and to be free – not just human beings either; dogs and spiders and trees and all other living beings as well. I do squash mosquitoes, but I am very, very sorry.

I received a wonderful document of comments and questions from a husband and wife couple, John and Rosanna. It made me laugh with delight when I read John's account of their discussion of my text, because their words brought so vividly before me the people themselves with their eager, perceptive approach to life. Here is one of the comments he noted (I include first the particular passage in the book to which he is referring)

The first principle is that there is a pattern to life: it is orderly, not random. 'Chance', 'luck', 'happenstance', 'mere coincidence' are interpretations put upon events by people with an incomplete grasp of what is happening to them, and an unwillingness or inability to create a habit of seeing what we believe instead of believing what we see.

Rosanna believes that it is sometimes a matter of luck if you stay healthy or not. She objects that the statement above is not falsifiable.

Falsifiable, no; verifiable, yes. My whole proposal in writing this book is that you give it a try. I believe that all disturbances of health have a spiritual and emotional component. How could they not? Our being is not compartmentalized. It's like having a No Smoking area in a restaurant or a No Peeing area in a swimming pool. Can't be done. Therefore the avenues of healing are numerous. However it gets there – call it luck, call it mismanagement, call it the gift of God – adversity certainly does show up in our lives; this is true for all of us. For most of us, some of the adversity will be health issues. Following the road of blessing gives us a template to start re-patterning the chaos, allowing us to take the loose threads of the torn fabric of our lives and join them back into something to be proud of, strengthening and enhancing. Even people following the road of blessing get overwhelmed, but they know what to do about it. It puzzles me that a person should believe in God and belong to Jesus but simultaneously believe that what happens to us can be a matter of luck. There is no room for luck in my understanding of how life works. It is all gift.

Rosanna says 'I always thought the bad things didn't come from God, but he allows them to happen. He gives you strength to get through them.'

Isaiah 45:7 says, 'I [God] bring prosperity and create disaster' (NIV), or 'I make peace, and create evil' (KJV). I believe that is true. And I agree with Rosanna that God gives us the strength to get through the testing times.

John wants to know 'why are we not taught that the Bible is weird?' It's usually a big old book in a big old building, it appears to be all about authority and conservatism (the establishment). The church is the establishment. But actually the Bible is subversive and strange and hard to understand. It doesn't get treated like that.

Weird is a good word. The ancient Celts believed that behind and beyond the mundane reality of everyday was the realm of Weird, the transformative supernatural realm, and that sometimes it broke through or we stumbled upon it. Yes, the Bible is weird. It is powerful, it speaks, it is transformative. It is a vessel of the supernatural realm. It carries God's word to us potently. The church is made up of people, and people are weak and corrupt. Those who are thirsty for power have seen the chance the Bible offers them to manipulate others by force and terror. They use the Bible to their own ends to bludgeon others into submission, they pick and choose from it to shape the religious establishment. They annex its authority to subjugate other people to their own ends, their own empire. Oscar Wilde said, 'I wrote when I did not know life. Now that I do know life, I know that life cannot be written, it can only be lived.' Those words give us a clue to the strangeness of the Bible. It is a book of life, and it becomes understandable when you live it. And yes, it is very subversive:

> My soul proclaims the greatness of the Lord, and my
> spirit has rejoiced in God my saviour…he has deposed
> those who occupied the seats of power and lifted up the
> disregarded, insignificant people of no account.
>
> *Luke 1:46–52 (my paraphrase)*

The woman who brought up Jesus said that, in one of her political protest songs.

And I agree the Bible is hard to understand. You have to start with the bits that are easy to understand, like this:

> Beloved, let us love one another, for love is of God, and
> everyone that loves is born of God and knows God.
> Whoever does not love does not know God, for God is
> love… Beloved, if God so loved us, we ought also to love
> one another… And we have known and believed God's
> love for us. God is love; and he that makes his home in
> love makes his home in God, and God in him… There's
> no fear in love; perfect love casts out fear: because fear
> has torment. He that is frightened has not yet been loved
> into wholeness. We love, because God first loved us. If
> someone says, 'I love God,' and hates his brother, he is a
> liar: for how can someone who doesn't love his brother,
> whom he has seen, love God whom he has never seen?
> And this commandment we have we from him, that he
> who loves God love his brother too.
>
> *(from 1 John 4, my paraphrase of the KJV)*

This is not hard to understand. If some bits seem too difficult and that worries you, start with that easy bit. When you have mastered it – by which I mean, when you have integrated its teaching into your life and you can do it – move on to another easy bit. Come to the difficult bits when you are more experienced at living the Bible.

One of my readers asked me questions so searching that it would take too much space to address them here. She did not finish reading the book – found my whole approach infuriating and baffling. I wish I could include all her questions here; here's just one of them. It is addressed to my assertion that in reading the Bible we do well to stay inside the text; setting ourselves above the text as judges robs us of its power.

To what extent is it possible – and desirable – to 'stay inside the text'? All words have shades of meaning acquired by a variety of usage, and we all bring different associations and experiences of language to our reading. These come from outside the text. We learn words and language outside of the text. We of necessity bring a wider understanding of the world to our reading, in the same way as we do in conversation, because language makes no sense without this. When we interact with another person, we go outside of their words to use our knowledge of the person, and the context, to interpret what they are saying. Why would we not use these cognitive skills – which God has given us – when interacting with God?

When I said that we should stay inside the text, I mean that we should work within the story offered us. For example, if we are studying the story of Adam and Eve, I think it is not helpful to us to ask questions like: 'Were these real individuals or mythical representatives of the human race?' 'Did Adam have a navel?' 'Was the Garden of Eden a real place?' 'Did God really create the world in seven days or is that part of the mythological language of the story?' I have my own thoughts about all those questions, but they are not of real relevance. In reading the Bible to strengthen my spirit and lead me in the path of righteousness, all I need to know is what's there in the Bible. I also take heed that we are to love the Lord our God with all our heart, *mind* and strength, so we do well to bring our cognitive skills to the scriptures. You can see from the way I have written about the Bible in the last chapter of the book that I find it helpful to analyze and understand the scriptures, understanding as best I can what each writer intends and means, and how that fits in with our lives: but I try never to set myself above the text, saying 'Jesus didn't really say that,' or 'He said the man was possessed of a demon but of course we know that was just their primitive language for psychiatric illness and demons don't really exist.' I respect the story. I respect the text.

Do you believe that if someone's bills are not paid, they are not walking in the way of blessing? How do you explain the lives of millions people in Third World countries who never have enough to eat, and die young of starvation or disease? Would you say they are not walking in the way of blessing?

I have no comment to make on how people got to where they are at the moment, only on the way forward that will help them wherever they are. I know that adversities happen to all of us, in some cases deep and terrible and as a direct result of their goodness: for example, people can be arrested and tortured for their faith or for sheltering others. What I am recommending here is not a divine insurance policy that will insulate us against adverse experiences, but a way to manage all experience, comfortable or painful, so as to achieve the best outcome from those circumstances. I do think that the question of starvation in the world has come to the human community because of our corporate mismanagement even where it is not caused by individual and personal mismanagement. I think we have the information readily available to us to prevent starvation and radically reduce disease. If we ate a primarily vegan diet, cared for the earth (intelligently using what we have found out about greenhouse gases, climate change etc), nurtured forests and waters, refrained from war and lived simply, we would have set the conditions for well-being throughout creation and including humankind. None of these things are difficult: they just require self-discipline. If some of us are starving, I would not necessarily say *they* are not walking in the road of blessing, but I would certainly say *we* are not walking in the road of blessing, and if we care about those starving people we should rectify that immediately.

You tell us 'not to believe everything we are told, or accept pre-packaged ideologies'. Why then should we believe what you are telling us to do?

In the preamble to this friend's list of questions, she also explained: 'I guess I expect a reason why I should believe this person, more than just that they feel they know it in their inmost being. If I were a stranger reading this book, as opposed to someone who knows you, there would be no reason for me to trust what your inmost being is telling you.'

I once saw a police drama on UK TV in which the detective hero (I forget which one it was) taught his subordinate a principle called the ABC rule, which I liked very much. The ABC stood for:

Assume nothing
Believe nothing
Check everything

I wholeheartedly concur with that. I have written this book about the road of blessing not at all for the sole reason that I believe it in my inmost being (though I do). I have written it because I have been following the road of blessing to the best of my poor ability for several decades now, and I *know* that what I am saying is true. Christian readers might also be inclined to believe what I am saying because these principles are all biblical: not in the sense of being supported by odd little proof texts here and there, but being foundational to the thinking and claims and assertions of the whole Bible. For those who believe in the authority of the Bible I would expect that to count as a reason to believe me.

In the Methodist church they have this wonderful thing called the 'Wesley Quadrilateral' – the four building bricks of faith. They are: Scripture (both Testaments of the Bible), Tradition (the accumulated testimony of the church over two thousand years), Experience (what my own life can personally testify), Reason (what analysis and reflection can tell me). I like to apply all these areas of wisdom to understanding and making sense of life, finding my way to something trustworthy and true. I recommend others to do the same. I believe that, especially if you persevere and read the book all the way through, and take time to live with the holistic sense of what I have said for a while, you will find it works.

But most of all, I recommend that you give it a try. Test it out; not for a week but for a year. Keep a journal. Often I pray for things but forget that I asked, so fail to notice when they are answered. I suffered badly from a frozen shoulder that was intensely painful. The regular routes of anti-inflammatories, cortisone injections, osteopathic manipulation or surgery did not appeal to me, and what I had read and observed suggested them to be of limited and unreliable benefit. So I took the problem to the Lord, explaining to him that I would like a healer, someone who could reach in and touch the root of the problem and give me enough help to get well again. A little time went by and I waited patiently, managing as best as I could. Then one day I was conducting a funeral at a town some miles away from home, and found to my surprise among the congregation a dear friend, one of what I call the 'kindred' (those who understand and walk in the road of faith and blessing). She asked me how I was. To most people I should have smiled and said 'Fine, thank you,' for that is always true: but I told her about my shoulder. Straight from the funeral she whisked me away for a therapeutic treatment, the first of several which have brought massive improvement and relief. If I hadn't remembered that I had prayed (and it's amazing how we can forget), of course I wouldn't notice the connection. So if you are testing it out, a journal can be helpful.

But don't believe anything just because I say it; I don't expect that of you at all! I have a sense of responsibility pressing upon me though, which is why I have written the book; I think it would be mean of me to keep it all to myself when I know that it's true.

In Celebration of Simplicity
by Penelope Wilcock

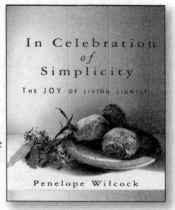

This practical yet visionary book offers a model for a truly healthy life based on gospel simplicity. Ditch the stuff that gets in the way, and your heart is free to respond to God.

'What an illuminating book! Pen goes right to the heart of the gospel with her rich understanding of what it means to walk the road of simplicity. Living lightly allows space for people, fun, prayer – all the good things of life.'
— **Dr Elaine Storkey**

'I have always admired Pen's writing. She has an immense talent for putting words together in the most effective possible way. This book invites the reader to join her in a fascinating journey of thought and sentiment. Don't worry about agreeing or disagreeing – just go. A wonderful collection of quotes will accompany you.'
— **Adrian Plass**

ISBN: 978-1-85424-912-8   £8.99
Available from your local Christian bookshop.
In case of difficulty, please visit our website:
www.lionhudson.com